Cram101 Textbook Outlines to accompany:

Best of Game Programming Gems

Mark DeLoura, 1st Edition

A Content Technologies Inc. publication (c) 2012.

STUDYING MADE EASY

This Craml0l notebook is designed to make studying easier and increase your comprehension of the textbook material. Instead of starting with a blank notebook and trying to write down everything discussed in class lectures, you can use this Craml01 textbook notebook and annotate your notes along with the lecture.

Our goal is to give you the best tools for success.

For a supreme understanding of the course, pair your notebook with our online tools. Should you decide you prefer Craml0l.com as your study tool,

we'd like to offer you a trade...

Our Trade In program is a simple way for us to keep our promise and provide you the best studying tools, regardless of where you purchased your Craml0l textbook notebook. As long as your notebook is in *Like New Condition**, you can send it back to us and we will immediately give you a Craml0l.com account free for 120 days!

Let The Trade In Begin!

THREE SIMPLE STEPS TO TRADE:

1. Go to www.cram101.com/tradein and fill out the packing slip information.

2. Submit and print the packing slip and mail it in with your Craml0l textbook notebook.

3. Activate your account after you receive your email confirmation.

* Books must be returned in *Like New Condition*, meaning there is no damage to the book including, but not limited to; ripped or torn pages, markings or writing on pages, or folded / creased pages. Upon receiving the book, Craml0l will inspect it and reserves the right to terminate your free Craml0l.com account and return your textbook notebook at the owners expense.

Learning System

Cram101 Textbook Outlines is a learning system. The notes in this book are the highlights of your textbook, you will never have to highlight a book again.

How to use this book. Take this book to class, it is your notebook for the lecture. The notes and highlights on the left hand side of the pages follow the outline and order of the textbook. All you have to do is follow along while your instructor presents the lecture. Circle the items emphasized in class and add other important information on the right side. With Cram101 Textbook Outlines you'll spend less time writing and more time listening. Learning becomes more efficient.

Cram101.com Online

Increase your studying efficiency by using Cram101.com's practice tests and online reference material. It is the perfect complement to Cram101 Textbook Outlines. Use self-teaching matching tests or simulate in-class testing with comprehensive multiple choice tests, or simply use Cram's true and false tests for quick review. Cram101.com even allows you to enter your in-class notes for an integrated studying format combining the textbook notes with your class notes.

Visit **www.Cram101.com**, click Sign Up at the top of the screen, and enter **DK73DW10400** in the promo code box on the registration screen. Your access to www.Cram101.com is discounted by 50% because you have purchased this book. Sign up and stop highlighting textbooks forever.

Best of Game Programming Gems
Mark DeLoura, 1st

CONTENTS

Clam101

Chapter 1. GENERAL INFORMATION

Maple	Maple is a general-purpose commercial computer algebra system. It was first developed in 1980 by the Symbolic Computation Group at the University of Waterloo in Waterloo, Ontario, Canada.
	Since 1988, it has been developed and sold commercially by Waterloo Maple Inc.
Protocol	In object-oriented programming, a protocol is what or how unrelated objects use to communicate with each other. These are definitions of methods and values which the objects agree upon in order to cooperate.
	For example, in Java (where protocols are termed interfaces), the `Comparable` interface specifies a method `compareTo` which implementing classes should implement.
Debugging	Debugging is a methodical process of finding and reducing the number of bugs, or defects, in a computer program or a piece of electronic hardware, thus making it behave as expected. Debugging tends to be harder when various subsystems are tightly coupled, as changes in one may cause bugs to emerge in another.
	Origin
	There is some controversy over the origin of the term 'debugging.'
	The terms 'bug' and 'debugging' are both popularly attributed to Admiral Grace Hopper in the 1940s.
Operator	Programming languages generally support a set of operators that are similar to operations in mathematics. A language may contain a fixed number of built-in operators (e.g. + - * = in C and C++), or it may allow the creation of programmer-defined operators (e.g. Haskell). Some programming languages restrict operator symbols to special characters like + or := while others allow also names like `div` (e.g. Pascal).

Chapter 1. GENERAL INFORMATION

Subprogram	In computer science, a subroutine is a portion of code within a larger program, which performs a specific task and is relatively independent of the remaining code. As the name 'subprogram' suggests, a subroutine behaves in much the same way as a computer program that is used as one step in a larger program or another subprogram. A subroutine is often coded so that it can be started ('called') several times and/or from several places during a single execution of the program, including from other subroutines, and then branch back (return) to the next instruction after the 'call' once the subroutine's task is done.
OpenMP	OpenMP is an application programming interface (API) that supports multi-platform shared memory multiprocessing programming in C, C++, and Fortran on many architectures, including Unix and Microsoft Windows platforms. It consists of a set of compiler directives, library routines, and environment variables that influence run-time behavior. Jointly defined by a group of major computer hardware and software vendors, OpenMP is a portable, scalable model that gives programmers a simple and flexible interface for developing parallel applications for platforms ranging from the desktop to the supercomputer.
Mersenne twister	The Mersenne twister is a pseudorandom number generator developed in 1997 by Makoto Matsumoto (?? ?$^?$) and Takuji Nishimura (?? ??$^?$) that is based on a matrix linear recurrence over a finite binary field F_2. It provides for fast generation of very high-quality pseudorandom numbers, having been designed specifically to rectify many of the flaws found in older algorithms. There are at least two common variants of the algorithm, differing only in the size of the Mersenne primes used.
Method	In object-oriented programming, a method is a subroutine that is exclusively associated either with a class (in which case it is called a class method is an instance method). Like a subroutine in procedural programming languages, a method usually consists of a sequence of programming statements to perform an action, a set of input parameters to customize those actions, and possibly an output value (called the return value) of some kind. Methods provide a mechanism for accessing and manipulating the encapsulated data stored in an object.

Chapter 1. GENERAL INFORMATION

Processing	Processing is an open source programming language and integrated development environment (IDE) built for the electronic arts and visual design communities with the purpose of teaching the basics of computer programming in a visual context, and to serve as the foundation for electronic sketchbooks. The project was initiated in 2001 by Casey Reas and Ben Fry, both formerly of the Aesthetics and Computation Group at the MIT Media Lab. One of the stated aims of Processing is to act as a tool to get non-programmers started with programming, through the instant gratification of visual feedback.
Taylor series	In mathematics, a Taylor series is a representation of a function as an infinite sum of terms that are calculated from the values of the function's derivatives at a single point.
	The concept of a Taylor series was formally introduced by the English mathematician Brook Taylor in 1715. he Scottish mathematician Colin Maclaurin, who made extensive use of this special case of Taylor series in the 18th century.
Quicksort	Quicksort is a sorting algorithm developed by C. A. R. Hoare that, on average, makes $O(nlogn)$ (big O notation) comparisons to sort n items. In the worst case, it makes $O(n^2)$ comparisons, though if implemented correctly this behavior is rare. Typically, quicksort is significantly faster in practice than other $O(nlogn)$ algorithms, because its inner loop can be efficiently implemented on most architectures, and in most real-world data it is possible to make design choices that minimize the probability of requiring quadratic time.
ChecKing	ChecKing is a web application developed by optimyth intended for monitoring the quality of software development process and its results, that covers the needs of organizations that want to control software quality before it is put into production.
	To do that the tool follows the standard ISO/IEC 9126.
	The automated analysis include measures obtained from the software development process (activity, requirements, defects and changes) and analyzable software elements: project documentation, source code, test scripts, build scripts.

Chapter 1. GENERAL INFORMATION

Compiler	A compiler is a computer program (or set of programs) that transforms source code written in a programming language (the source language) into another computer language (the target language, often having a binary form known as object code). The most common reason for wanting to transform source code is to create an executable program.
	The name 'compiler' is primarily used for programs that translate source code from a high-level programming language to a lower level language (e.g., assembly language or machine code).
Class	In object-oriented programming, a class is a construct that is used as a blueprint (or template) to create objects of that class. This blueprint describes the state and behavior that the objects of the class all share. An object of a given class is called an instance of the class.
Arithmetic	arithmetic s is the oldest and most elementary branch of mathematics, used by almost everyone, for tasks ranging from simple day-to-day counting to advanced science and business calculations. It involves the study of quantity, especially as the result of combining numbers. In common usage, it refers to the simpler properties when using the traditional operations of addition, subtraction, multiplication and division with smaller values of numbers.
Index	In computer science, an index can be:

1. an integer which identifies an array element
2. a data structure that enables sublinear-time lookup

Array element identifier

When data objects are stored in an array, individual objects are selected by an index which is usually a non-negative scalar integer. Indices are also called subscripts.

Chapter 1. GENERAL INFORMATION

There are three ways in which the elements of an array can be indexed:

0 (zero-based indexing)
>The first element of the array is indexed by subscript of 0.

1 (one-based indexing)
>The first element of the array is indexed by subscript of 1.

n (n-based indexing)
>The base index of an array can be freely chosen.

ASSIST

ASSIST is an IBM System/370-compatible assembler and interpreter developed in the 1970s at Penn State University by John Mashey and a group of Mashey's student assistants. Originally, ASSIST was available only to universities and was implemented at several hundred of them, but was occasionally used elsewhere. In 1998, Penn State declared that ASSIST was no longer copyrighted and that the program was freely available.

Engine

An engine is a continuation-based construct that provides timed preemption. Engines which can contain other engines are sometimes called nesters and engines which don't have this ability are then called flat engines. To implement timed preemption there needs to be a clock.

Navigation

Navigation is the process of monitoring and controlling the movement of a craft or vehicle from one place to another. It is also the term of art used for the specialized knowledge used by navigators to perform navigation tasks. All navigational techniques involve locating the navigator's position compared to known locations or patterns.

Variable

In computer programming, a variable is a symbolic name given to some known or unknown quantity or information, for the purpose of allowing the name to be used independently of the information it represents. A variable name in computer source code is usually associated with a data storage location and thus also its contents, and these may change during the course of program execution.

Variables in programming may not directly correspond to the concept of variables in mathematics.

Chapter 1. GENERAL INFORMATION

Macro	A macro in computer science is a rule or pattern that specifies how a certain input sequence (often a sequence of characters) should be mapped to an output sequence (also often a sequence of characters) according to a defined procedure. The mapping process that instantiates (transforms) a macro into a specific output sequence is known as macro expansion. The term originated with macro-assemblers, where the idea is to make available to the programmer a sequence of computing instructions as a single program statement, making the programming task less tedious and less error-prone.
String	In formal languages, which are used in mathematical logic and theoretical computer science, a string is a finite sequence of symbols that are chosen from a set or alphabet. In computer programming, a string is, essentially, a sequence of characters. A string is generally understood as a data type storing a sequence of data values, usually bytes, in which elements usually stand for characters according to a character encoding, which differentiates it from the more general array data type.
Element	Boolean logic is a complete system for logical operations, used in many systems. It was named after George Boole, who first defined an algebraic system of logic in the mid 19th century. Boolean logic(or 'bits') each contain only two possible values, called various names, such as 'true' and 'false', 'yes' and 'no', 'on' and 'off', or '1' and '0'. Let X be a set: · An element is one member of a set.
Lighting	Lighting is the deliberate application of light to achieve some aesthetic or practical effect. Lighting includes use of both artificial light sources such as lamps and natural illumination of interiors from daylight. Daylighting.

Chapter 1. GENERAL INFORMATION

Numbers	Numbers is a spreadsheet application developed by Apple Inc. as part of the iWork productivity suite alongside Keynote and Pages. Numbers 1.0 was announced on August 7, 2007 and thus it is the newest application in the iWork Suite.
Shadow	A shadow is an area where direct light from a light source cannot reach due to obstruction by an object. It occupies all of the space behind an opaque object with light in front of it. The cross section of a shadow is a two-dimensional silhouette, or reverse projection of the object blocking the light.
Speech recognition	Speech recognition converts spoken words to text. The term 'voice recognition' is sometimes used to refer to recognition systems that must be trained to a particular speaker--as is the case for most desktop recognition software. Recognizing the speaker can simplify the task of translating speech.
Infinite loop	An infinite loop is a sequence of instructions in a computer program which loops endlessly, either due to the loop having no terminating condition, having one that can never be met, or one that causes the loop to start over. In older operating systems with cooperative multitasking, infinite loops normally caused the entire system to become unresponsive. With the now-prevalent preemptive multitasking model, infinite loops usually cause the program to consume all available processor time, but can usually be terminated by the user.
Interface	In the field of computer science, an interface refers to a point of interaction between components, and is applicable at the level of both hardware and software. This allows a component, whether a piece of hardware such as a graphics card or a piece of software such as an internet browser, to function independently while using interfaces to communicate with other components via an input/output system and an associated protocol. In addition to hardware and software interfaces, a computing interface may refer to the means of communication between the computer and the user by means of peripheral devices such a monitor or a keyboard, an interface with the internet via Internet Protocol, and any other point of communication involving a computer.
Inline function	In various versions of the C and C++ programming languages, an inline function is a function that the compiler has been requested to perform inline expansion upon. In other words, the programmer has requested that the compiler insert the complete body of the function in every place that the function is called, rather than generating code to call the function in the one place it is defined. (However, compilers are not obligated to respect this request).

Chapter 1. GENERAL INFORMATION

Cache	In computer engineering, a cache is a component that transparently stores data so that future requests for that data can be served faster. The data that is stored within a cache might be values that have been computed earlier or duplicates of original values that are stored elsewhere. If requested data is contained in the cache this request can be served by simply reading the cache, which is comparatively faster. Otherwise (cache miss), the data has to be recomputed or fetched from its original storage location, which is comparatively slower. Hence, the more requests can be served from the cache the faster the overall system performance is.
Keyword	Keywords are the words that are used to reveal the internal structure of an author's reasoning. While they are used primarily for rhetoric, they are also used in a strictly grammatical sense for structural composition, reasoning, and comprehension. Indeed, they are an essential part of any language.
Copying	Copying is the duplication of information or an artifact based only on an instance of that information or artifact, and not using the process that originally generated it. With analog forms of information, copying is only possible to a limited degree of accuracy, which depends on the quality of the equipment used and the skill of the operator. With digital forms of information, perfect copying is not only possible, but is, almost by definition, the norm.
BASIC	In computer programming, BASIC is a family of high-level programming languages. The original BASIC was designed in 1964 by John George Kemeny and Thomas Eugene Kurtz at Dartmouth College in New Hampshire, USA to provide computer access to non-science students. At the time, nearly all use of computers required writing custom software, which was something only scientists and mathematicians tended to be able to do.
Implementation	Implementation is the realization of an application, idea, model, design, specification, standard, algorithm, or policy.

In computer science, an implementation(computer science)

· Programming language implementation

· Algorithm

· Application software

· Code

· Computation

· Function

· Method

· Process

· Proceeding

· Procedure

· Scheme

· Solution

· System

· Technique

'.

Component Object Model

Component Object Model is a binary-interface standard for software componentry introduced by Microsoft in 1993. It is used to enable interprocess communication and dynamic object creation in a large range of programming languages. The term Component Object Model is often used in the Microsoft software development industry as an umbrella term that encompasses the OLE, OLE Automation, ActiveX, Component Object Model+ and DCOM technologies.

Overview

The essence of Component Object Model is a language-neutral way of implementing objects that can be used in environments different from the one in which they were created, even across machine boundaries.

IUnknown

In programming, the IUnknown interface is the fundamental interface in the Component Object Model (COM). The published COM specification mandates that COM objects must minimally implement this interface. Furthermore, every other COM interface must be derived from IUnknown.

Chapter 1. GENERAL INFORMATION

Identification	The function of identification is to map a known quantity to an unknown entity so as to make it known. The known quantity is called the identifier (or ID) and the unknown entity is what needs identification. A basic requirement for identification is that the ID be unique.
Object model	In computing, object model has two related but distinct meanings: 1. The properties of objects in general, in a specific computer programming language, technology, notation or methodology that uses them. For example, the Java object model, the COM object model, or the object model of OMT. Such object models are usually defined using concepts such as class, message, inheritance, polymorphism, and encapsulation. There is an extensive literature on formalized object models as a subset of the formal semantics of programming languages. 2. A collection of objects or classes through which a program can examine and manipulate some specific parts of its world.
Pointer	In computer science, a pointer is a programming language data type whose value refers directly to (or 'points to') another value stored elsewhere in the computer memory using its address. For high-level programming languages, pointers effectively take the place of general purpose registers in low-level languages such as assembly language or machine code, but may be in available memory. A pointer references a location in memory, and obtaining the value at the location a pointer refers to is known as dereferencing the pointer.
Resource	In the Java programming language a resource is a piece of data that can be accessed by the code of an application. An application can access its resources through Uniform Resource Locators, like web resources, but the resources are usually contained within the JAR file(s) of the application. A resource bundle is a set of key and value pairs, stored as a resource, that is commonly used to allow the localization of an application.
Handle	In computer programming, a handle is a particular kind of smart pointer. Handles are used when an application references blocks of memory or objects managed by another system, such as a database or an operating system.

Chapter 1. GENERAL INFORMATION

While a pointer literally contains the address of the item to which it refers, a handle is an abstract reference controlled by a separate system; its opacity allows the referent to be relocated in memory by the system without invalidating the handle - impossible with pointers.

Polynomial	In mathematics, a polynomial is an expression of finite length constructed from variables (also known as indeterminates) and constants, using only the operations of addition, subtraction, multiplication, and non-negative integer exponents. For example, $x^2 - 4x + 7$ is a polynomial, but $x^2 - 4/x + 7x^{3/2}$ is not, because its second term involves division by the variable x (4/x) and because its third term contains an exponent that is not a whole number (3/2). The term 'polynomial' indicates a simplified algebraic form such that all polynomials are similarly simple in complexity (cf.
Smart pointer	In computer science, a smart pointer is an abstract data type that simulates a pointer while providing additional features, such as automatic garbage collection or bounds checking. These additional features are intended to reduce bugs caused by the misuse of pointers while retaining efficiency. Smart pointers typically keep track of the objects they point to for the purpose of memory management.
Weak reference	In computer programming, a weak reference is a reference that does not protect the referenced object from collection by a garbage collector. An object referenced only by weak references is considered unreachable (or 'weakly reachable') and so may be collected at any time. Weak references are used to avoid keeping memory references by unneeded objects.
Container	In computer science, a container is a class, a data structure, or an abstract data type (ADT) whose instances are collections of other objects. In other words; They are used for storing objects in an organized way following specific access rules.

Generally, container classes are expected to implement methods to do the following:

- create a new empty container
- report the number of objects it stores (size),
- delete all the objects in the container
- insert new objects into the container,
- remove objects from it,
- provide access to the stored objects.`

Chapter 1. GENERAL INFORMATION

There are two types of containers: value containers and reference containers.

Queue	A queue in British English refers to a line, usually of people, cars etc., assembled in the order they arrived and waiting for some event or service. The next person to be served is the person at the front of the queue. New arrivals go to the back of the queue.
Terminology	Terminology is the study of terms and their use. Terms are words and compound words that are used in specific contexts. Not to be confused with 'terms' in colloquial usages, the shortened form of technical terms (or terms of art) which are defined within a discipline or speciality field.
Algorithm	In mathematics, computer science, and other areas, an algorithm is an effective method for solving a problem expressed as a finite sequence of steps. Algorithms are used for calculation, data processing, and many other fields. .
Iterator	In computer science, an iterator is an object that allows a programmer to traverse through all the elements of a collection, regardless of its specific implementation. An iterator is sometimes called a cursor, especially within the context of a database. Description External iterators and the iterator pattern An external iterator may be thought of as a type of pointer that has two primary operations: referencing one particular element in the object collection (called element access), and modifying itself so it points to the next element (called element traversal).
Linked list	In computer science, a linked list is a data structure that consists of a sequence of nodes each of which contains a reference (i.e., a link) to the next node in the sequence.

Chapter 1. GENERAL INFORMATION

Linked lists are among the simplest and most common data structures. They can be used to implement several other common abstract data structures, including stacks, queues, associative arrays, and symbolic expressions, though it is not uncommon to implement the other data structures directly without using a list as the basis of implementation.

Naming convention	In computer programming, a naming convention is a set of rules for choosing the character sequence to be used for identifiers which denote variables, types and functions etc. in source code and documentation.
	Reasons for using a naming convention include the following:
	• to reduce the effort needed to read and understand source code;
	• to enhance source code appearance (for example, by disallowing overly long names or abbreviations).
	The choice of naming conventions can be an enormously controversial issue, with partisans of each holding theirs to be the best and others to be inferior.
Collision	In computer science, a collision is a situation that occurs when two distinct pieces of data have the same hash value, checksum, fingerprint, or cryptographic digest.
	Collisions are unavoidable whenever members of a very large set (such as all possible person names, or all possible computer files) are mapped to a relatively short bit string. This is merely an instance of the pigeonhole principle.
Binary tree	In computer science, a binary tree is a tree data structure in which each node has at most two child nodes, usually distinguished as 'left' and 'right'. Nodes with children are parent nodes, and child nodes may contain references to their parents. Outside the tree, there is often a reference to the 'root' node (the ancestor of all nodes), if it exists.

Chapter 1. GENERAL INFORMATION

Red-black tree	A Red-black tree is a type of self-balancing binary search tree, a data structure used in computer science, typically used to implement associative arrays. The original structure was invented in 1972 by Rudolf Bayer who called them 'symmetric binary B-trees', but acquired its modern name in a paper in 1978 by Leonidas J. Guibas and Robert Sedgewick. It is complex, but has good worst-case running time for its operations and is efficient in practice: it can search, insert, and delete in O(log n) time, where n is total number of elements in the tree.
Collision detection	Collision detection typically refers to the computational problem of detecting the intersection of two or more objects. While the topic is most often associated with its use in video games and other physical simulations, it also has applications in robotics. In addition to determining whether two objects have collided, collision detection systems may also calculate time of impact (TOI), and report a contact manifold (the set of intersecting points).
Typedef	`typedef` is a keyword in the C and C++ programming languages. The purpose of `typedef` is to assign alternative names to existing types, most often those whose standard declaration is cumbersome, potentially confusing, or likely to vary from one implementation to another. Under C convention (such as in the C standard library), types declared with typedef end with '_t' (e.g., size_t, time_t).
Template	Technical overview There are two kinds of templates: function templates and class templates. Function templates A function template behaves like a function except that the template can have arguments of many different types . In other words, a function template represents a family of functions.

Clam101

Chapter 1. GENERAL INFORMATION

Comparison

In computer programming, comparison of two data items is effected by the comparison operators typically written as:

> (greater than)
< (less than)
>= (greater than or equal to)
<= (less than or equal to)
= or == (exactly equal to)
!=, <>, ~= or /= (not equal to)

These operators produce the logical value `true` or `false`, depending on the result of the comparison. For example, in the pseudo-code

```
if a > 1 then ...
```

the statements following `then` are executed only if the value of the variable 'a' is greater than 1 (i.e. when the logical value of `a > 1` is `true`).

Some programming languages make a syntactical distinction between the 'equals' of assignment (e.g. `a = 1` assigns the value 1 to the variable 'a') and the 'equals' of comparison.

Optimization

In mathematics, computer science and economics, optimization, refers to choosing the best element from some set of available alternatives.

In the simplest case, this means solving problems in which one seeks to minimize or maximize a real function by systematically choosing the values of real or integer variables from within an allowed set. This formulation, using a scalar, real-valued objective function, is probably the simplest example; the generalization of optimization theory and techniques to other formulations comprises a large area of applied mathematics.

CIam101

Function object

A function object, functional, or functionoid, is a computer programming construct allowing an object to be invoked or called as though it were an ordinary function, usually with the same syntax.

Description

A typical use of a function object is in writing callback functions. A callback in procedural languages, such as C, may be performed by using function pointers.

Virtual function

In object-oriented programming, a virtual function is a function or method whose behaviour can be overridden within an inheriting class by a function with the same signature. This concept is a very important part of the polymorphism portion of object-oriented programming (OOP).

Purpose

The concept of the virtual function solves the following problem:

In OOP when a derived class inherits a base class, an object of the derived class may be referred to (or cast) as either being the base class type or the derived class type.

Size

Size is a command line utility originally written for use with the Unix-like operating systems. It processes one or more ELF files and its output are the dimensions (in bytes) of the text, data and uninitialized sections, and their total.

Common use:

$ size ...

Here follows some examples on Solaris (/usr/ccs/bin/size); options and syntax may vary on different Operating Systems:

$ size /usr/ccs/bin/size9066 + 888 + 356 = 10310

With -f option name and size of each section are printed out, plus their total:

$ size -f /usr/ccs/bin/size17(.interp) + 636(.hash) + 1440(.dynsym) + 743(.dynstr) + 64 (.SUNW_version) + 48(.rela.ex_shared) + 24(.rela.bss) + 336(.rela.plt) + 4760(.text) +80(.init) + 80(.fini) + 4(.exception_ranges) + 28(.rodata) + 590(.rodata1) + 12(.got) + 388(.plt) + 192 (.dynamic) + 40(.ex_shared) + 112(.data) +140(.data1) + 352(.bss) = 10086

With -F option size and permission flag of each sections are printed out, plus their total:

$ size -F /usr/ccs/bin/size9066(r-x) + 1244(rwx) = 10470

.

Vorbis

Vorbis is a free software / open source project headed by the Xiph.Org Foundation (formerly Xiphophorus company). The project produces an audio format specification and software implementation (codec) for lossy audio compression. Vorbis is most commonly used in conjunction with the Ogg container format and it is therefore often referred to as Ogg Vorbis.

Feature

In computer vision and image processing the concept of feature is used to denote a piece of information which is relevant for solving the computational task related to a certain application. More specifically, features can refer to

- the result of a general neighborhood operation (feature extractor or feature detector) applied to the image,
- specific structures in the image itself, ranging from simple structures such as points or edges to more complex structures such as objects.

Other examples of features are related to motion in image sequences, to shapes defined in terms of curves or boundaries between different image regions, or to properties of such a region.

The feature concept is very general and the choice of features in a particular computer vision system may be highly dependent on the specific problem at hand.

Profiling

In software engineering, program profiling, software profiling, a form of dynamic program analysis (as opposed to static code analysis), is the investigation of a program's behavior using information gathered as the program executes. The usual purpose of this analysis is to determine which sections of a program to optimize - to increase its overall speed, decrease its memory requirement or sometimes both.

- A (code) profiler is a performance analysis tool that, most commonly, measures only the frequency and duration of function calls, but there are other specific types of profilers (e.g. memory profilers) in addition to more comprehensive profilers, capable of gathering extensive performance data.
- An instruction set simulator which is also -- by necessity -- a profiler, can measure the totality of a program's behaviour from invocation to termination.

Gathering program events

Profilers use a wide variety of techniques to collect data, including hardware interrupts, code instrumentation, instruction set simulation, operating system hooks, and performance counters.

Parameter

In computer programming, a parameter is a special kind of variable, used in a subroutine to refer to one of the pieces of data provided as input to the subroutine.. These pieces of data are called arguments. An ordered list of parameters is usually included in the definition of a subroutine, so that, each time the subroutine is called, its arguments for that call can be assigned to the corresponding parameters.

Node	A node is an abstract basic unit used to build linked data structures such as trees, linked lists, and computer-based representations of graphs. Each node contains some data and possibly links to other nodes. Links between nodes are often implemented by pointers or references.
Thread	In computer science, a thread of execution is the smallest unit of processing that can be scheduled by an operating system. It generally results from a fork of a computer program into two or more concurrently running tasks. The implementation of threads and processes differs from one operating system to another, but in most cases, a thread is contained inside a process.

Chapter 2. MATH AND PHYSICS.

Protocol	In object-oriented programming, a protocol is what or how unrelated objects use to communicate with each other. These are definitions of methods and values which the objects agree upon in order to cooperate. For example, in Java (where protocols are termed interfaces), the `Comparable` interface specifies a method `compareTo` which implementing classes should implement.
Quicksort	Quicksort is a sorting algorithm developed by C. A. R. Hoare that, on average, makes $O(n\log n)$ (big O notation) comparisons to sort n items. In the worst case, it makes $O(n^2)$ comparisons, though if implemented correctly this behavior is rare. Typically, quicksort is significantly faster in practice than other $O(n\log n)$ algorithms, because its inner loop can be efficiently implemented on most architectures, and in most real-world data it is possible to make design choices that minimize the probability of requiring quadratic time.
Approximation	An approximation is an inexact representation of something that is still close enough to be useful. Although approximation is most often applied to numbers, it is also frequently applied to such things as mathematical functions, shapes, and physical laws. Approximations may be used because incomplete information prevents use of exact representations.
Taylor series	In mathematics, a Taylor series is a representation of a function as an infinite sum of terms that are calculated from the values of the function's derivatives at a single point. The concept of a Taylor series was formally introduced by the English mathematician Brook Taylor in 1715. he Scottish mathematician Colin Maclaurin, who made extensive use of this special case of Taylor series in the 18th century.
Algorithm	In mathematics, computer science, and other areas, an algorithm is an effective method for solving a problem expressed as a finite sequence of steps. Algorithms are used for calculation, data processing, and many other fields. .

Chapter 2. MATH AND PHYSICS.

Range	In computer science, the term range may refer to one of three things: 1. The possible values that may be stored in a variable. 2. The upper and lower bounds of an array. 3. An alternative to iterator. Range of a variable The range of a variable is given as the set of possible values that that variable can hold. In the case of an integer, the variable definition is restricted to whole numbers only, and the range will cover every number within its range. For example, the range of a signed 16-bit integer variable is all the integers from −32,768 to +32,767.
Polynomial	In mathematics, a polynomial is an expression of finite length constructed from variables (also known as indeterminates) and constants, using only the operations of addition, subtraction, multiplication, and non-negative integer exponents. For example, $x^2 - 4x + 7$ is a polynomial, but $x^2 - 4/x + 7x^{3/2}$ is not, because its second term involves division by the variable x (4/x) and because its third term contains an exponent that is not a whole number (3/2). The term 'polynomial' indicates a simplified algebraic form such that all polynomials are similarly simple in complexity (cf.
Compiler	A compiler is a computer program (or set of programs) that transforms source code written in a programming language (the source language) into another computer language (the target language, often having a binary form known as object code). The most common reason for wanting to transform source code is to create an executable program. The name 'compiler' is primarily used for programs that translate source code from a high-level programming language to a lower level language (e.g., assembly language or machine code).
Inline function	In various versions of the C and C++ programming languages, an inline function is a function that the compiler has been requested to perform inline expansion upon. In other words, the programmer has requested that the compiler insert the complete body of the function in every place that the function is called, rather than generating code to call the function in the one place it is defined. (However, compilers are not obligated to respect this request).

Chapter 2. MATH AND PHYSICS.

Minimax	Minimax is a decision rule used in decision theory, game theory, statistics and philosophy for minimizing the possible loss while maximizing the potential gain. Alternatively, it can be thought of as maximizing the minimum gain (maximin). Originally formulated for two-player zero-sum game theory, covering both the cases where players take alternate moves and those where they make simultaneous moves, it has also been extended to more complex games and to general decision making in the presence of uncertainty.
Method	In object-oriented programming, a method is a subroutine that is exclusively associated either with a class (in which case it is called a class method is an instance method). Like a subroutine in procedural programming languages, a method usually consists of a sequence of programming statements to perform an action, a set of input parameters to customize those actions, and possibly an output value (called the return value) of some kind. Methods provide a mechanism for accessing and manipulating the encapsulated data stored in an object.
OpenMP	OpenMP is an application programming interface (API) that supports multi-platform shared memory multiprocessing programming in C, C++, and Fortran on many architectures, including Unix and Microsoft Windows platforms. It consists of a set of compiler directives, library routines, and environment variables that influence run-time behavior.
	Jointly defined by a group of major computer hardware and software vendors, OpenMP is a portable, scalable model that gives programmers a simple and flexible interface for developing parallel applications for platforms ranging from the desktop to the supercomputer.
Collision	In computer science, a collision is a situation that occurs when two distinct pieces of data have the same hash value, checksum, fingerprint, or cryptographic digest.
	Collisions are unavoidable whenever members of a very large set (such as all possible person names, or all possible computer files) are mapped to a relatively short bit string. This is merely an instance of the pigeonhole principle.

Chapter 2. MATH AND PHYSICS.

Collision detection	Collision detection typically refers to the computational problem of detecting the intersection of two or more objects. While the topic is most often associated with its use in video games and other physical simulations, it also has applications in robotics. In addition to determining whether two objects have collided, collision detection systems may also calculate time of impact (TOI), and report a contact manifold (the set of intersecting points).
Numbers	Numbers is a spreadsheet application developed by Apple Inc. as part of the iWork productivity suite alongside Keynote and Pages. Numbers 1.0 was announced on August 7, 2007 and thus it is the newest application in the iWork Suite.
Optimization	In mathematics, computer science and economics, optimization, refers to choosing the best element from some set of available alternatives. In the simplest case, this means solving problems in which one seeks to minimize or maximize a real function by systematically choosing the values of real or integer variables from within an allowed set. This formulation, using a scalar, real-valued objective function, is probably the simplest example; the generalization of optimization theory and techniques to other formulations comprises a large area of applied mathematics.
Arithmetic	arithmetic s is the oldest and most elementary branch of mathematics, used by almost everyone, for tasks ranging from simple day-to-day counting to advanced science and business calculations. It involves the study of quantity, especially as the result of combining numbers. In common usage, it refers to the simpler properties when using the traditional operations of addition, subtraction, multiplication and division with smaller values of numbers.
SIMD	Single instruction, multiple data (SIMD), is a class of parallel computers in Flynn's taxonomy. It describes computers with multiple processing elements that perform the same operation on multiple data simultaneously. Thus, such machines exploit data level parallelism.
Interpolation	In the mathematical subfield of numerical analysis, interpolation is a method of constructing new data points within the range of a discrete set of known data points.

Chapter 2. MATH AND PHYSICS.

In engineering and science one often has a number of data points, as obtained by sampling or experimentation, and tries to construct a function which closely fits those data points. This is called curve fitting or regression analysis.

Slerp	In computer graphics, Slerp is shorthand for spherical linear interpolation, introduced by Ken Shoemake in the context of quaternion interpolation for the purpose of animating 3D rotation. It refers to constant speed motion along a unit radius great circle arc, given the ends and an interpolation parameter between 0 and 1.
	Geometric Slerp
	Slerp has a geometric formula independent of quaternions, and independent of the dimension of the space in which the arc is embedded.
Maple	Maple is a general-purpose commercial computer algebra system. It was first developed in 1980 by the Symbolic Computation Group at the University of Waterloo in Waterloo, Ontario, Canada.
	Since 1988, it has been developed and sold commercially by Waterloo Maple Inc.
Mersenne twister	The Mersenne twister is a pseudorandom number generator developed in 1997 by Makoto Matsumoto (?? ?[?]) and Takuji Nishimura (?? ??[?]) that is based on a matrix linear recurrence over a finite binary field F_2. It provides for fast generation of very high-quality pseudorandom numbers, having been designed specifically to rectify many of the flaws found in older algorithms. There are at least two common variants of the algorithm, differing only in the size of the Mersenne primes used.
Subprogram	In computer science, a subroutine is a portion of code within a larger program, which performs a specific task and is relatively independent of the remaining code.

Chapter 2. MATH AND PHYSICS.

As the name 'subprogram' suggests, a subroutine behaves in much the same way as a computer program that is used as one step in a larger program or another subprogram. A subroutine is often coded so that it can be started ('called') several times and/or from several places during a single execution of the program, including from other subroutines, and then branch back (return) to the next instruction after the 'call' once the subroutine's task is done.

Object model

In computing, object model has two related but distinct meanings:

1. The properties of objects in general, in a specific computer programming language, technology, notation or methodology that uses them. For example, the Java object model, the COM object model, or the object model of OMT. Such object models are usually defined using concepts such as class, message, inheritance, polymorphism, and encapsulation. There is an extensive literature on formalized object models as a subset of the formal semantics of programming languages.
2. A collection of objects or classes through which a program can examine and manipulate some specific parts of its world.

Class

In object-oriented programming, a class is a construct that is used as a blueprint (or template) to create objects of that class. This blueprint describes the state and behavior that the objects of the class all share. An object of a given class is called an instance of the class.

Command-line interface

A command-line interface is a mechanism for interacting with a computer operating system or software by typing commands to perform specific tasks. This text-only interface contrasts with the use of a mouse pointer with a graphical user interface (GUI) to click on options, or menus on a text user interface (TUI) to select options. This method of instructing a computer to perform a given task is referred to as 'entering' a command: the system waits for the user to conclude the submitting of the text command by pressing the 'Enter' key (a descendant of the 'carriage return' key of a typewriter keyboard).

Interface

In the field of computer science, an interface refers to a point of interaction between components, and is applicable at the level of both hardware and software. This allows a component, whether a piece of hardware such as a graphics card or a piece of software such as an internet browser, to function independently while using interfaces to communicate with other components via an input/output system and an associated protocol.

In addition to hardware and software interfaces, a computing interface may refer to the means of communication between the computer and the user by means of peripheral devices such a monitor or a keyboard, an interface with the internet via Internet Protocol, and any other point of communication involving a computer.

Operator

Programming languages generally support a set of operators that are similar to operations in mathematics. A language may contain a fixed number of built-in operators (e.g. + - * = in C and C++), or it may allow the creation of programmer-defined operators (e.g. Haskell). Some programming languages restrict operator symbols to special characters like + or := while others allow also names like `div` (e.g. Pascal).

Inverse kinematics

The inverse kinematics problem is simply stated as, 'Given the desired position of the robot's hand, what must be the angles at all of the robot's joints?' This is in contrast to the forward kinematics problem, which is, 'Given the angles at all of the robot's joints, what is the position of the hand?'

Humans solve the inverse kinematics problem constantly without conscious effort. For example, when eating cereal in the morning, humans reach out for their spoons without consciously considering the relative configuration of their shoulder and elbow required to reach the spoon.

Physics

Kinematics is the formal description of motion.

Implementation

Implementation is the realization of an application, idea, model, design, specification, standard, algorithm, or policy.

In computer science, an implementation(computer science)

· Programming language implementation

· Algorithm

· Application software

· Code

· Computation

· Function

· Method

· Process

· Proceeding

· Procedure

· Scheme

· Solution

· System

· Technique

'.

Generator | In computer science, a generator is a special routine that can be used to control the iteration behaviour of a loop. A generator is very similar to a function that returns an array, in that a generator has parameters, can be called, and generates a sequence of values. However, instead of building an array containing all the values and returning them all at once, a generator yields the values one at a time, which requires less memory and allows the caller to get started processing the first few values immediately.

Chapter 2. MATH AND PHYSICS.

Pseudorandom number generator	A pseudorandom number generator also known as a deterministic random bit generator (DRBG), is an algorithm for generating a sequence of numbers that approximates the properties of random numbers. The sequence is not truly random in that it is completely determined by a relatively small set of initial values, called the PRNG's state. Although sequences that are closer to truly random can be generated using hardware random number generators, pseudorandom numbers are important in practice for simulations (e.g., of physical systems with the Monte Carlo method), and are central in the practice of cryptography and procedural generation.
Floating point	In computing, floating point describes a system for representing numbers that would be too large or too small to be represented as integers. Numbers are in general represented approximately to a fixed number of significant digits and scaled using an exponent. The base for the scaling is normally 2, 10 or 16. The typical number that can be represented exactly is of the form: $$\text{significant digits} \times \text{base}^{\text{exponent}}$$ The term floating point refers to the fact that the radix point (decimal point, or, more commonly in computers, binary point) can 'float'; that is, it can be placed anywhere relative to the significant digits of the number.
Integer	In computer science, the term integer is used to refer to a data type which represents some finite subset of the mathematical integers. These are also known as integral data types. Value and representation The value of a datum with an integral type is the mathematical integer that it corresponds to.
Least significant bit	In computing, the least significant bit is the bit position in a binary integer giving the units value, that is, determining whether the number is even or odd. The lsb is sometimes referred to as the right-most bit, due to the convention in positional notation of writing less significant digits further to the right. It is analogous to the least significant digit of a decimal integer, which is the digit in the ones (right-most) position.

Chapter 2. MATH AND PHYSICS.

Processing	Processing is an open source programming language and integrated development environment (IDE) built for the electronic arts and visual design communities with the purpose of teaching the basics of computer programming in a visual context, and to serve as the foundation for electronic sketchbooks. The project was initiated in 2001 by Casey Reas and Ben Fry, both formerly of the Aesthetics and Computation Group at the MIT Media Lab. One of the stated aims of Processing is to act as a tool to get non-programmers started with programming, through the instant gratification of visual feedback.
BASIC	In computer programming, BASIC is a family of high-level programming languages. The original BASIC was designed in 1964 by John George Kemeny and Thomas Eugene Kurtz at Dartmouth College in New Hampshire, USA to provide computer access to non-science students. At the time, nearly all use of computers required writing custom software, which was something only scientists and mathematicians tended to be able to do.
Engine	An engine is a continuation-based construct that provides timed preemption. Engines which can contain other engines are sometimes called nesters and engines which don't have this ability are then called flat engines. To implement timed preemption there needs to be a clock.
Pipeline	In software engineering, a pipeline consists of a chain of processing elements (processes, threads, coroutines, etc). arranged so that the output of each element is the input of the next. Usually some amount of buffering is provided between consecutive elements. The information that flows in these pipelines is often a stream of records, bytes or bits.
Index	In computer science, an index can be:

1. an integer which identifies an array element
2. a data structure that enables sublinear-time lookup

Array element identifier

When data objects are stored in an array, individual objects are selected by an index which is usually a non-negative scalar integer. Indices are also called subscripts.

Chapter 2. MATH AND PHYSICS.

There are three ways in which the elements of an array can be indexed:

0 (zero-based indexing)
> The first element of the array is indexed by subscript of 0.

1 (one-based indexing)
> The first element of the array is indexed by subscript of 1.

n (n-based indexing)
> The base index of an array can be freely chosen.

PATH

PATH is an environment variable on Unix-like operating systems, DOS, OS/2, and Microsoft Windows, specifying a set of directories where executable programs are located. In general, each executing process or user session has its own PATH setting.

Unix and Unix-like

On POSIX and Unix-like operating systems, the `$PATH` variable is specified as a list of one or more directory names separated by colon (`:`) characters.

Resolution

In mathematical logic and automated theorem proving, resolution is a rule of inference leading to a refutation theorem-proving technique for sentences in propositional logic and first-order logic. In other words, iteratively applying the resolution rule in a suitable way allows for telling whether a propositional formula is satisfiable and for proving that a first-order formula is unsatisfiable; this method may prove the satisfiability of a first-order satisfiable formula, but not always, as it is the case for all methods for first-order logic. Resolution was introduced by John Alan Robinson in 1965.

Constraint

In mathematics, a constraint is a condition that a solution to an optimization problem must satisfy. There are two types of constraints: equality constraints and inequality constraints. The set of solutions that satisfy all constraints is called the feasible set.

Block

In computer programming, a block is a section of code which is grouped together. Blocks consist of one or more declarations and statements. A programming language that permits the creation of blocks, including blocks nested within other blocks, is called a block structured programming language.

Chapter 2. MATH AND PHYSICS.

Friction

Friction is the force resisting the relative motion of solid surfaces, fluid layers, and/or material elements sliding against each other. There are several types of friction:

- Dry friction resists relative lateral motion of two solid surfaces in contact. Dry friction is subdivided into static friction between non-moving surfaces, and kinetic friction between moving surfaces.

- Fluid friction describes the friction between layers within a viscous fluid that are moving relative to each other.

- Lubricated friction is a case of fluid friction where a fluid separates two solid surfaces.

- Skin friction is a component of drag, the force resisting the motion of a solid body through a fluid.

- Internal friction is the force resisting motion between the elements making up a solid material while it undergoes deformation.

When surfaces in contact move relative to each other, the friction between the two surfaces converts kinetic energy into heat.

Node

A node is an abstract basic unit used to build linked data structures such as trees, linked lists, and computer-based representations of graphs. Each node contains some data and possibly links to other nodes. Links between nodes are often implemented by pointers or references.

Class	In object-oriented programming, a class is a construct that is used as a blueprint (or template) to create objects of that class. This blueprint describes the state and behavior that the objects of the class all share. An object of a given class is called an instance of the class.
Method	In object-oriented programming, a method is a subroutine that is exclusively associated either with a class (in which case it is called a class method is an instance method). Like a subroutine in procedural programming languages, a method usually consists of a sequence of programming statements to perform an action, a set of input parameters to customize those actions, and possibly an output value (called the return value) of some kind. Methods provide a mechanism for accessing and manipulating the encapsulated data stored in an object.
Optimization	In mathematics, computer science and economics, optimization, refers to choosing the best element from some set of available alternatives.
	In the simplest case, this means solving problems in which one seeks to minimize or maximize a real function by systematically choosing the values of real or integer variables from within an allowed set. This formulation, using a scalar, real-valued objective function, is probably the simplest example; the generalization of optimization theory and techniques to other formulations comprises a large area of applied mathematics.
PATH	PATH is an environment variable on Unix-like operating systems, DOS, OS/2, and Microsoft Windows, specifying a set of directories where executable programs are located. In general, each executing process or user session has its own PATH setting.
	Unix and Unix-like
	On POSIX and Unix-like operating systems, the $PATH variable is specified as a list of one or more directory names separated by colon (:) characters.
Protocol	In object-oriented programming, a protocol is what or how unrelated objects use to communicate with each other. These are definitions of methods and values which the objects agree upon in order to cooperate.

For example, in Java (where protocols are termed interfaces), the `Comparable` interface specifies a method `compareTo` which implementing classes should implement.

Synchronization	Synchronization is timekeeping which requires the coordination of events to operate a system in unison. The familiar conductor of an orchestra serves to keep the orchestra in time. Systems operating with all their parts in synchrony are said to be synchronous or in sync.
OpenMP	OpenMP is an application programming interface (API) that supports multi-platform shared memory multiprocessing programming in C, C++, and Fortran on many architectures, including Unix and Microsoft Windows platforms. It consists of a set of compiler directives, library routines, and environment variables that influence run-time behavior.
	Jointly defined by a group of major computer hardware and software vendors, OpenMP is a portable, scalable model that gives programmers a simple and flexible interface for developing parallel applications for platforms ranging from the desktop to the supercomputer.
Macro	A macro in computer science is a rule or pattern that specifies how a certain input sequence (often a sequence of characters) should be mapped to an output sequence (also often a sequence of characters) according to a defined procedure. The mapping process that instantiates (transforms) a macro into a specific output sequence is known as macro expansion.
	The term originated with macro-assemblers, where the idea is to make available to the programmer a sequence of computing instructions as a single program statement, making the programming task less tedious and less error-prone.

Index	In computer science, an index can be:
	
	1. an integer which identifies an array element
	2. a data structure that enables sublinear-time lookup
	
	Array element identifier
	
	When data objects are stored in an array, individual objects are selected by an index which is usually a non-negative scalar integer. Indices are also called subscripts.
	
	There are three ways in which the elements of an array can be indexed:
	
	0 (zero-based indexing)
	    The first element of the array is indexed by subscript of 0.
	1 (one-based indexing)
	    The first element of the array is indexed by subscript of 1.
	n (n-based indexing)
	    The base index of an array can be freely chosen.

Partitioning	Generally, a partition is a splitting of something into parts. The term is used in a variety of senses: · Partition (law), to divide up a piece of land into separate portions representing the proportionate interests of the tenants. It may also consist of dividing a property with common ownership into identifiable individual ownership · Batch processing: splitting of a single batch job over a large number of processors. · Disk partitioning: organization of a disk on PC systems

· RTOS or IMA partitioning: In the case of Integrated Modular Avionics and the use of Real-Time Operating Systems, there are at least four types of partitioning often required: spatial partitioning, temporal partitioning, control partitioning and resource partitioning. Using these techniques, high integrity processes are protected from other, or low integrity, processes.

· Hardware Partition, such as IBM LPAR or SUN Logical Domains

· Logical partition: division of a physical memory into protected areas

· Partition (database): division of a database into parts

· List of partition topics

· Partition of a set, a collection of non-empty subsets such that every element belongs to one and only one of the subsets

· Partition (number theory), a way to write a positive integer as a sum of other positive integers; the partition function gives the number of different ways to partition a number

· Multiplicative partition, a way to write an integer greater than 1 as a product of other integers that are also greater than 1.

· Partition problem, an NP-complete problem: given a set of integers, can the set be partitioned into two subsets with equal sums?

· A partition of unity is a set of functions whose sum is the constant function

· Partition of an interval, used in the theory of the Riemann integral and the Riemann-Stieltjes integral

· Partition (music) -- a method of creating segments from sets when the twelve-tone technique is used

· Partition (1987 film)

· Partition (2007 film)

· Partition function (statistical mechanics)

· Partition function (quantum field theory)

· Partition coefficient

· Partition (politics)
Notable examples are:

· Partitions of Poland and Poland-Lithuania in the 18th, 19th and 20th centuries

· 1905 Partition of Bengal and 1947 Partition of Bengal

· Partition of India (colonial British India) in 1947 into the independent dominions (later republics) of India and Pakistan (which included modern day Bangladesh)

· Partition of Punjab in 1966 into the states of Punjab, Haryana and Himachal Pradesh

· Partition of Pakistan in 1971, when East Pakistan became the independent nation of Bangladesh after the Bangladesh Liberation War

· 1947 UN Partition Plan for Palestine (region)

· Partition of Ireland in 1920 into the independent Irish Free State and Northern Ireland

· Treaty of Kars of 1921, which partitioned Ottoman Armenia between the republic of Turkey and the then Soviet Union (Western and Eastern Armenia)

· Partition of Vietnam in 1954

· Partitions of Luxembourg, last in 1838 into Duchy of Luxembourg and Belgian province

· The hypothetical partition of the Canadian province of Quebec

· Office partitions, which may be used to form cubicles

· Folding screens such as ByÅ　bu

· Industrial partitions generally constructed of wire mesh panels. These wire partitions are used to separate and/or secure different zones within an industrial manufacturing or distribution facility.

Quicksort	Quicksort is a sorting algorithm developed by C. A. R. Hoare that, on average, makes O(nlogn) (big O notation) comparisons to sort n items. In the worst case, it makes $O(n^2)$ comparisons, though if implemented correctly this behavior is rare. Typically, quicksort is significantly faster in practice than other O(nlogn) algorithms, because its inner loop can be efficiently implemented on most architectures, and in most real-world data it is possible to make design choices that minimize the probability of requiring quadratic time.
Engine	An engine is a continuation-based construct that provides timed preemption. Engines which can contain other engines are sometimes called nesters and engines which don't have this ability are then called flat engines. To implement timed preemption there needs to be a clock.
Polygon	In geometry a polygon is traditionally a plane figure that is bounded by a closed path or circuit, composed of a finite sequence of straight line segments (i.e., by a closed polygonal chain). These segments are called its edges or sides, and the points where two edges meet are the polygon's vertices or corners. An n-gon is a polygon with n sides.
Quadtree	A quadtree is a tree data structure in which each internal node has exactly four children. Quadtrees are most often used to partition a two dimensional space by recursively subdividing it into four quadrants or regions. The regions may be square or rectangular, or may have arbitrary shapes.
Visibility	Visibility is a mathematical abstraction of the real-life notion of visibility. Given a set of obstacles in the Euclidean space, two points in the space are said to be visible to each other, if the line segment that joins them does not intersect any obstacles.

Computation of visibility is among the basic problems in computational geometry and finds applications in computer graphics, motion planning, and other areas.

| Collision | In computer science, a collision is a situation that occurs when two distinct pieces of data have the same hash value, checksum, fingerprint, or cryptographic digest.

Collisions are unavoidable whenever members of a very large set (such as all possible person names, or all possible computer files) are mapped to a relatively short bit string. This is merely an instance of the pigeonhole principle.

| Collision detection | Collision detection typically refers to the computational problem of detecting the intersection of two or more objects. While the topic is most often associated with its use in video games and other physical simulations, it also has applications in robotics. In addition to determining whether two objects have collided, collision detection systems may also calculate time of impact (TOI), and report a contact manifold (the set of intersecting points).

| Processing | Processing is an open source programming language and integrated development environment (IDE) built for the electronic arts and visual design communities with the purpose of teaching the basics of computer programming in a visual context, and to serve as the foundation for electronic sketchbooks. The project was initiated in 2001 by Casey Reas and Ben Fry, both formerly of the Aesthetics and Computation Group at the MIT Media Lab. One of the stated aims of Processing is to act as a tool to get non-programmers started with programming, through the instant gratification of visual feedback.

| Spline | In mathematics, a spline is a special function defined piecewise by polynomials. In interpolating problems, spline interpolation is often preferred to polynomial interpolation because it yields similar results, even when using low-degree polynomials, while avoiding Runge's phenomenon for higher degrees.

In computer science subfields of computer-aided design and computer graphics, the term 'spline' more frequently refers to a piecewise polynomial (parametric) curve.

Compiler	A compiler is a computer program (or set of programs) that transforms source code written in a programming language (the source language) into another computer language (the target language, often having a binary form known as object code). The most common reason for wanting to transform source code is to create an executable program. The name 'compiler' is primarily used for programs that translate source code from a high-level programming language to a lower level language (e.g., assembly language or machine code).
Instance	In object-oriented programming an instance is an occurrence or a copy of an object, whether currently executing or not. Instances of a class share the same set of attributes, yet will typically differ in what those attributes contain. For example, a class 'Employee' would describe the attributes common to all instances of the Employee class.
Resource	In the Java programming language a resource is a piece of data that can be accessed by the code of an application. An application can access its resources through Uniform Resource Locators, like web resources, but the resources are usually contained within the JAR file(s) of the application. A resource bundle is a set of key and value pairs, stored as a resource, that is commonly used to allow the localization of an application.
Field	In computer science, data that has several parts can be divided into fields. For Relational databases arrange data as sets of database records, also called rows. Each record consists of several fields; the fields of all records form the columns.
Algorithm	In mathematics, computer science, and other areas, an algorithm is an effective method for solving a problem expressed as a finite sequence of steps. Algorithms are used for calculation, data processing, and many other fields. .
Hash table	In computer science, a hash table is a data structure that uses a hash function to map identifying values, known as keys (e.g., a person's name), to their associated values (e.g., their telephone number). Thus, a hash table implements an associative array. The hash function is used to transform the key into the index (the hash) of an array element (the slot or bucket) where the corresponding value is to be sought.

Chapter 3. ARTIFICIAL INTELLIGE

Node	A node is an abstract basic unit used to build linked data structures such as trees, linked lists, and computer-based representations of graphs. Each node contains some data and possibly links to other nodes. Links between nodes are often implemented by pointers or references.
Table	In relational databases and flat file databases, a table is a set of data elements (values) that is organized using a model of vertical columns (which are identified by their name) and horizontal rows. A table has a specified number of columns, but can have any number of rows. Each row is identified by the values appearing in a particular column subset which has been identified as a candidate key.
Mersenne twister	The Mersenne twister is a pseudorandom number generator developed in 1997 by Makoto Matsumoto (?? ?') and Takuji Nishimura (?? ???') that is based on a matrix linear recurrence over a finite binary field F_2. It provides for fast generation of very high-quality pseudorandom numbers, having been designed specifically to rectify many of the flaws found in older algorithms. There are at least two common variants of the algorithm, differing only in the size of the Mersenne primes used.
Queue	A queue in British English refers to a line, usually of people, cars etc., assembled in the order they arrived and waiting for some event or service. The next person to be served is the person at the front of the queue. New arrivals go to the back of the queue.
Polynomial	In mathematics, a polynomial is an expression of finite length constructed from variables (also known as indeterminates) and constants, using only the operations of addition, subtraction, multiplication, and non-negative integer exponents. For example, $x^2 - 4x + 7$ is a polynomial, but $x^2 - 4/x + 7x^{3/2}$ is not, because its second term involves division by the variable x (4/x) and because its third term contains an exponent that is not a whole number (3/2). The term 'polynomial' indicates a simplified algebraic form such that all polynomials are similarly simple in complexity (cf.
Taylor series	In mathematics, a Taylor series is a representation of a function as an infinite sum of terms that are calculated from the values of the function's derivatives at a single point. The concept of a Taylor series was formally introduced by the English mathematician Brook Taylor in 1715. he Scottish mathematician Colin Maclaurin, who made extensive use of this special case of Taylor series in the 18th century.

Navigation	Navigation is the process of monitoring and controlling the movement of a craft or vehicle from one place to another. It is also the term of art used for the specialized knowledge used by navigators to perform navigation tasks. All navigational techniques involve locating the navigator's position compared to known locations or patterns.
Round-off error	A round-off error, is the difference between the calculated approximation of a number and its exact mathematical value. Numerical analysis specifically tries to estimate this error when using approximation equations and/or algorithms, especially when using finitely many digits to represent real numbers (which in theory have infinitely many digits). This is a form of quantization error.
Constraint	In mathematics, a constraint is a condition that a solution to an optimization problem must satisfy. There are two types of constraints: equality constraints and inequality constraints. The set of solutions that satisfy all constraints is called the feasible set.
Range	In computer science, the term range may refer to one of three things: 1. The possible values that may be stored in a variable. 2. The upper and lower bounds of an array. 3. An alternative to iterator. Range of a variable The range of a variable is given as the set of possible values that that variable can hold. In the case of an integer, the variable definition is restricted to whole numbers only, and the range will cover every number within its range. For example, the range of a signed 16-bit integer variable is all the integers from −32,768 to +32,767.
Lighting	Lighting is the deliberate application of light to achieve some aesthetic or practical effect. Lighting includes use of both artificial light sources such as lamps and natural illumination of interiors from daylight. Daylighting.
Shadow	A shadow is an area where direct light from a light source cannot reach due to obstruction by an object. It occupies all of the space behind an opaque object with light in front of it. The cross section of a shadow is a two-dimensional silhouette, or reverse projection of the object blocking the light.

Character	In computer and machine-based telecommunications terminology, a character is a unit of information that roughly corresponds to a grapheme, grapheme-like unit, or symbol, such as in an alphabet or syllabary in the written form of a natural language.
	Examples of characters include letters, numerical digits, and common punctuation marks (such as '.' or '-'). The concept also includes control characters, which do not correspond to symbols in a particular natural language, but rather to other bits of information used to process text in one or more languages.
Vorbis	Vorbis is a free software / open source project headed by the Xiph.Org Foundation (formerly Xiphophorus company). The project produces an audio format specification and software implementation (codec) for lossy audio compression. Vorbis is most commonly used in conjunction with the Ogg container format and it is therefore often referred to as Ogg Vorbis.
Variable	In computer programming, a variable is a symbolic name given to some known or unknown quantity or information, for the purpose of allowing the name to be used independently of the information it represents. A variable name in computer source code is usually associated with a data storage location and thus also its contents, and these may change during the course of program execution.
	Variables in programming may not directly correspond to the concept of variables in mathematics.

Object model	In computing, object model has two related but distinct meanings: 1. The properties of objects in general, in a specific computer programming language, technology, notation or methodology that uses them. For example, the Java object model, the COM object model, or the object model of OMT. Such object models are usually defined using concepts such as class, message, inheritance, polymorphism, and encapsulation. There is an extensive literature on formalized object models as a subset of the formal semantics of programming languages. 2. A collection of objects or classes through which a program can examine and manipulate some specific parts of its world.
Local variables	In computer science, a local variable is a variable that is given local scope. Such a variable is accessible only from the function or block in which it is declared. Local variables are contrasted with global variables.
Negation	In logic and mathematics, Negation is an operation on propositions. For example, in classical logic Negation is normally interpreted by the truth function that takes truth to falsity and vice versa. In intuitionistic logic, according to the Brouwer-Heyting-Kolmogorov interpretation, the Negation of a proposition P is the proposition whose proofs are the refutations of P.
Operator	Programming languages generally support a set of operators that are similar to operations in mathematics. A language may contain a fixed number of built-in operators (e.g. + - * = in C and C++), or it may allow the creation of programmer-defined operators (e.g. Haskell). Some programming languages restrict operator symbols to special characters like + or := while others allow also names like `div` (e.g. Pascal).
Precondition	In computer programming, a precondition is a condition or predicate that must always be true just prior to the execution of some section of code or before an operation in a formal specification. If a precondition is violated, the effect of the section of code becomes undefined and thus may or may not carry out its intended work. Security problems can arise due to incorrect preconditions.

Planner	Planner is a programming language designed by Carl Hewitt at MIT, and first published in 1969. First, subsets such as Micro-Planner and Pico-Planner were implemented, and then essentially the whole language was implemented in Popler. Derivations such as QA4, Conniver, QLISP and Ether were important tools in Artificial Intelligence research in the 1970s, which influenced commercial developments such as KEE and ART.

Procedural Approach versus Logical Approach

The two major paradigms for constructing semantic software systems were procedural and logical. The procedural paradigm was epitomized by Lisp [McCarthy et al. 1962] which featured recursive procedures that operated on list structures.

Game engine	A game engine is a system designed for the creation and development of video games. There are many game engines that are designed to work on video game consoles and personal computers. The core functionality typically provided by a game engine includes a rendering engine ('renderer') for 2D or 3D graphics, a physics engine or collision detection (and collision response), sound, scripting, animation, artificial intelligence, networking, streaming, memory management, threading, localization support, and a scene graph.

Chapter 4. GRAPHICS

Class	In object-oriented programming, a class is a construct that is used as a blueprint (or template) to create objects of that class. This blueprint describes the state and behavior that the objects of the class all share. An object of a given class is called an instance of the class.
Polygon	In geometry a polygon is traditionally a plane figure that is bounded by a closed path or circuit, composed of a finite sequence of straight line segments (i.e., by a closed polygonal chain). These segments are called its edges or sides, and the points where two edges meet are the polygon's vertices or corners. An n-gon is a polygon with n sides.
Engine	An engine is a continuation-based construct that provides timed preemption. Engines which can contain other engines are sometimes called nesters and engines which don't have this ability are then called flat engines. To implement timed preemption there needs to be a clock.
Method	In object-oriented programming, a method is a subroutine that is exclusively associated either with a class (in which case it is called a class method is an instance method). Like a subroutine in procedural programming languages, a method usually consists of a sequence of programming statements to perform an action, a set of input parameters to customize those actions, and possibly an output value (called the return value) of some kind. Methods provide a mechanism for accessing and manipulating the encapsulated data stored in an object.
Speech recognition	Speech recognition converts spoken words to text. The term 'voice recognition' is sometimes used to refer to recognition systems that must be trained to a particular speaker--as is the case for most desktop recognition software. Recognizing the speaker can simplify the task of translating speech.
Arithmetic	arithmetic s is the oldest and most elementary branch of mathematics, used by almost everyone, for tasks ranging from simple day-to-day counting to advanced science and business calculations. It involves the study of quantity, especially as the result of combining numbers. In common usage, it refers to the simpler properties when using the traditional operations of addition, subtraction, multiplication and division with smaller values of numbers.
Mersenne twister	The Mersenne twister is a pseudorandom number generator developed in 1997 by Makoto Matsumoto (?? ?$^?$) and Takuji Nishimura (?? ??$^?$) that is based on a matrix linear recurrence over a finite binary field F_2. It provides for fast generation of very high-quality pseudorandom numbers, having been designed specifically to rectify many of the flaws found in older algorithms. There are at least two common variants of the algorithm, differing only in the size of the Mersenne primes used.

Chapter 4. GRAPHICS

Processing	Processing is an open source programming language and integrated development environment (IDE) built for the electronic arts and visual design communities with the purpose of teaching the basics of computer programming in a visual context, and to serve as the foundation for electronic sketchbooks. The project was initiated in 2001 by Casey Reas and Ben Fry, both formerly of the Aesthetics and Computation Group at the MIT Media Lab. One of the stated aims of Processing is to act as a tool to get non-programmers started with programming, through the instant gratification of visual feedback.
Skeleton	Skeleton programming is a style of computer programming based on simple high-level program structures and so called dummy code. Program skeletons resemble pseudocode, but allow parsing, compilation and testing of the code.
	Dummy code is inserted in a program skeleton to simulate processing and avoid compilation error messages.
Algorithm	In mathematics, computer science, and other areas, an algorithm is an effective method for solving a problem expressed as a finite sequence of steps. Algorithms are used for calculation, data processing, and many other fields. .
Quicksort	Quicksort is a sorting algorithm developed by C. A. R. Hoare that, on average, makes $O(nlogn)$ (big O notation) comparisons to sort n items. In the worst case, it makes $O(n^2)$ comparisons, though if implemented correctly this behavior is rare. Typically, quicksort is significantly faster in practice than other $O(nlogn)$ algorithms, because its inner loop can be efficiently implemented on most architectures, and in most real-world data it is possible to make design choices that minimize the probability of requiring quadratic time.

Chapter 4. GRAPHICS

Object model	In computing, object model has two related but distinct meanings: 1. The properties of objects in general, in a specific computer programming language, technology, notation or methodology that uses them. For example, the Java object model, the COM object model, or the object model of OMT. Such object models are usually defined using concepts such as class, message, inheritance, polymorphism, and encapsulation. There is an extensive literature on formalized object models as a subset of the formal semantics of programming languages. 2. A collection of objects or classes through which a program can examine and manipulate some specific parts of its world.
Motion capture	Motion capture, motion tracking, or mocap are terms used to describe the process of recording movement and translating that movement on to a digital model. It is used in military, entertainment, sports, and medical applications, and for validation of computer vision and robotics. In filmmaking it refers to recording actions of human actors, and using that information to animate digital character models in 2D or 3D computer animation.
Channel	Channels are a tool used for interprocess communication. An object may be sent over a channel, and a process is able to receive any objects sent over a channel it has a reference to. They are similar to pipelines, but may contain arbitrary unserialised objects instead of lines of text, and are used within a single program for coordination, rather than across several programs.
Numbers	Numbers is a spreadsheet application developed by Apple Inc. as part of the iWork productivity suite alongside Keynote and Pages. Numbers 1.0 was announced on August 7, 2007 and thus it is the newest application in the iWork Suite.
Organizing	organizing is the act of rearranging elements following one or more rules. Anything is commonly considered organized when it looks like everything has a correct order or placement. But it's only ultimately organized if any element has no difference on time taken to find it.
Identification	The function of identification is to map a known quantity to an unknown entity so as to make it known. The known quantity is called the identifier (or ID) and the unknown entity is what needs identification. A basic requirement for identification is that the ID be unique.

Chapter 4. GRAPHICS

Protocol	In object-oriented programming, a protocol is what or how unrelated objects use to communicate with each other. These are definitions of methods and values which the objects agree upon in order to cooperate. For example, in Java (where protocols are termed interfaces), the `Comparable` interface specifies a method `compareTo` which implementing classes should implement.
Interpolation	In the mathematical subfield of numerical analysis, interpolation is a method of constructing new data points within the range of a discrete set of known data points. In engineering and science one often has a number of data points, as obtained by sampling or experimentation, and tries to construct a function which closely fits those data points. This is called curve fitting or regression analysis.
Graphics	Graphics are visual presentations on some surface, such as a wall, canvas, computer screen, paper, inform, illustrate, or entertain. Examples are photographs, drawings, Line Art, graphs, diagrams, typography, numbers, symbols, geometric designs, maps, engineering drawings, or other images. graphics Drawing generally involves making marks on a surface by applying pressure from a tool, or moving a tool across a surface.
Inverse kinematics	The inverse kinematics problem is simply stated as, 'Given the desired position of the robot's hand, what must be the angles at all of the robot's joints?' This is in contrast to the forward kinematics problem, which is, 'Given the angles at all of the robot's joints, what is the position of the hand?' Humans solve the inverse kinematics problem constantly without conscious effort. For example, when eating cereal in the morning, humans reach out for their spoons without consciously considering the relative configuration of their shoulder and elbow required to reach the spoon. Physics

Kinematics is the formal description of motion.

Quadtree

A quadtree is a tree data structure in which each internal node has exactly four children. Quadtrees are most often used to partition a two dimensional space by recursively subdividing it into four quadrants or regions. The regions may be square or rectangular, or may have arbitrary shapes.

Sorting

Sorting is any process of arranging items in some sequence and/or in different sets, and accordingly, it has two common, yet distinct meanings:

1. ordering: arranging items of the same kind, class, nature, etc. in some ordered sequence,
2. categorizing: grouping and labeling items with similar properties together (by sorts).

Sorting information or data

For the sorting to be unique, these two are restricted to a total order and a strict total order, respectively.

Sorting n-tuples (depending on context also called e.g. records consisting of fields) can be done based on one or more of its components.

Approximation

An approximation is an inexact representation of something that is still close enough to be useful. Although approximation is most often applied to numbers, it is also frequently applied to such things as mathematical functions, shapes, and physical laws.

Approximations may be used because incomplete information prevents use of exact representations.

Chapter 4. GRAPHICS

Index	In computer science, an index can be:

1. an integer which identifies an array element
2. a data structure that enables sublinear-time lookup

Array element identifier

When data objects are stored in an array, individual objects are selected by an index which is usually a non-negative scalar integer. Indices are also called subscripts.

There are three ways in which the elements of an array can be indexed:

0 (zero-based indexing)
> The first element of the array is indexed by subscript of 0.

1 (one-based indexing)
> The first element of the array is indexed by subscript of 1.

n (n-based indexing)
> The base index of an array can be freely chosen.

Maple	Maple is a general-purpose commercial computer algebra system. It was first developed in 1980 by the Symbolic Computation Group at the University of Waterloo in Waterloo, Ontario, Canada.

Since 1988, it has been developed and sold commercially by Waterloo Maple Inc.

OpenMP	OpenMP is an application programming interface (API) that supports multi-platform shared memory multiprocessing programming in C, C++, and Fortran on many architectures, including Unix and Microsoft Windows platforms. It consists of a set of compiler directives, library routines, and environment variables that influence run-time behavior.

Jointly defined by a group of major computer hardware and software vendors, OpenMP is a portable, scalable model that gives programmers a simple and flexible interface for developing parallel applications for platforms ranging from the desktop to the supercomputer.

Taylor series

In mathematics, a Taylor series is a representation of a function as an infinite sum of terms that are calculated from the values of the function's derivatives at a single point.

The concept of a Taylor series was formally introduced by the English mathematician Brook Taylor in 1715. he Scottish mathematician Colin Maclaurin, who made extensive use of this special case of Taylor series in the 18th century.

Lighting

Lighting is the deliberate application of light to achieve some aesthetic or practical effect. Lighting includes use of both artificial light sources such as lamps and natural illumination of interiors from daylight. Daylighting.

Lookup table

In computer science, a lookup table is a data structure, usually an array or associative array, often used to replace a runtime computation with a simpler array indexing operation. The savings in terms of processing time can be significant, since retrieving a value from memory is often faster than undergoing an 'expensive' computation or input/output operation. The tables may be precalculated and stored in static program storage or calculated (or 'pre-fetched') as part of a programs initialization phase (memoization).

Subprogram

In computer science, a subroutine is a portion of code within a larger program, which performs a specific task and is relatively independent of the remaining code.

As the name 'subprogram' suggests, a subroutine behaves in much the same way as a computer program that is used as one step in a larger program or another subprogram. A subroutine is often coded so that it can be started ('called') several times and/or from several places during a single execution of the program, including from other subroutines, and then branch back (return) to the next instruction after the 'call' once the subroutine's task is done.

Shadow

A shadow is an area where direct light from a light source cannot reach due to obstruction by an object. It occupies all of the space behind an opaque object with light in front of it. The cross section of a shadow is a two-dimensional silhouette, or reverse projection of the object blocking the light.

Chapter 4. GRAPHICS

Table	In relational databases and flat file databases, a table is a set of data elements (values) that is organized using a model of vertical columns (which are identified by their name) and horizontal rows. A table has a specified number of columns, but can have any number of rows. Each row is identified by the values appearing in a particular column subset which has been identified as a candidate key.
Grayscale	In photography and computing, a grayscale or greyscale digital image is an image in which the value of each pixel is a single sample, that is, it carries only intensity information. Images of this sort, also known as black-and-white, are composed exclusively of shades of gray, varying from black at the weakest intensity to white at the strongest. grayscale images are distinct from one-bit black-and-white images, which in the context of computer imaging are images with only the two colors, black, and white (also called bilevel or binary images).
Interface	In the field of computer science, an interface refers to a point of interaction between components, and is applicable at the level of both hardware and software. This allows a component, whether a piece of hardware such as a graphics card or a piece of software such as an internet browser, to function independently while using interfaces to communicate with other components via an input/output system and an associated protocol. In addition to hardware and software interfaces, a computing interface may refer to the means of communication between the computer and the user by means of peripheral devices such a monitor or a keyboard, an interface with the internet via Internet Protocol, and any other point of communication involving a computer.
Operator	Programming languages generally support a set of operators that are similar to operations in mathematics. A language may contain a fixed number of built-in operators (e.g. + - * = in C and C++), or it may allow the creation of programmer-defined operators (e.g. Haskell). Some programming languages restrict operator symbols to special characters like + or := while others allow also names like `div` (e.g. Pascal).

Chapter 4. GRAPHICS

Radiance	Radiance and spectral radiance are radiometric measures that describe the amount of light that passes through or is emitted from a particular area, and falls within a given solid angle in a specified direction. They are used to characterize both emission from diffuse sources and reflection from diffuse surfaces. The SI unit of radiance is watts per steradian per square metre $(W \cdot sr^{-1} \cdot m^{-2})$.
Macro	A macro in computer science is a rule or pattern that specifies how a certain input sequence (often a sequence of characters) should be mapped to an output sequence (also often a sequence of characters) according to a defined procedure. The mapping process that instantiates (transforms) a macro into a specific output sequence is known as macro expansion.
	The term originated with macro-assemblers, where the idea is to make available to the programmer a sequence of computing instructions as a single program statement, making the programming task less tedious and less error-prone.
Solid	In computer programming, SOLID is a mnemonic acronym introduced by Robert C. Martin in the early 2000s which stands for five basic patterns of object-oriented programming and design. The principles when applied together make it much more likely that a programmer will create a system that is easy to maintain and extend over time. The principles of SOLID are guidelines that can be applied while working on software to remove code smells by causing the programmer to refactor the software's source code until it is both legible and extensible.
Surface	In mathematics, specifically in topology, a surface is a two-dimensional topological manifold. The most familiar examples are those that arise as the boundaries of solid objects in ordinary three-dimensional Euclidean space R^3 -- for example, the surface of a ball. On the other hand, there are surfaces, such as the Klein bottle, that cannot be embedded in three-dimensional Euclidean space without introducing singularities or self-intersections.
Polynomial	In mathematics, a polynomial is an expression of finite length constructed from variables (also known as indeterminates) and constants, using only the operations of addition, subtraction, multiplication, and non-negative integer exponents. For example, $x^2 - 4x + 7$ is a polynomial, but $x^2 - 4/x + 7x^{3/2}$ is not, because its second term involves division by the variable x (4/x) and because its third term contains an exponent that is not a whole number (3/2). The term 'polynomial' indicates a simplified algebraic form such that all polynomials are similarly simple in complexity (cf.

Chapter 4. GRAPHICS

Factor	Factor is a stack-oriented programming language created by Slava Pestov. Factor is dynamically typed and has automatic memory management, as well as powerful metaprogramming features. The language has a single implementation featuring a self-hosted optimizing compiler and an interactive development environment. The Factor distribution includes a large standard library.
Layer	In object-oriented design, a layer is a group of classes that have the same set of link-time module dependencies to other modules. In other words, a layer is a group of reusable components that are reusable in similar circumstances. In programming languages, the layer distinction is often expressed as 'import' dependencies between software modules.
Shading	Shading refers to depicting depth perception in 3D models or illustrations by varying levels of darkness.
	Drawing
	Shading is a process used in drawing for depicting levels of darkness on paper by applying media more densely or with a darker shade for darker areas, and less densely or with a lighter shade for lighter areas. There are various techniques of shading including cross hatching where perpendicular lines of varying closeness are drawn in a grid pattern to shade an area.
Pixel	In digital imaging, a pixel is a single point in a raster image. The pixel is the smallest addressable screen element; it is the smallest unit of picture that can be controlled. Each pixel has its own address.
BASIC	In computer programming, BASIC is a family of high-level programming languages. The original BASIC was designed in 1964 by John George Kemeny and Thomas Eugene Kurtz at Dartmouth College in New Hampshire, USA to provide computer access to non-science students. At the time, nearly all use of computers required writing custom software, which was something only scientists and mathematicians tended to be able to do.
Compiler	A compiler is a computer program (or set of programs) that transforms source code written in a programming language (the source language) into another computer language (the target language, often having a binary form known as object code). The most common reason for wanting to transform source code is to create an executable program.

	The name 'compiler' is primarily used for programs that translate source code from a high-level programming language to a lower level language (e.g., assembly language or machine code).
Billboard	A billboard is a large outdoor advertising structure (a billing board), typically found in high traffic areas such as alongside busy roads. Billboards present large advertisements to passing pedestrians and drivers. Typically showing large, ostensibly witty slogans, and distinctive visuals, billboards are highly visible in the top designated market areas.
Collision	In computer science, a collision is a situation that occurs when two distinct pieces of data have the same hash value, checksum, fingerprint, or cryptographic digest. Collisions are unavoidable whenever members of a very large set (such as all possible person names, or all possible computer files) are mapped to a relatively short bit string. This is merely an instance of the pigeonhole principle.
Collision detection	Collision detection typically refers to the computational problem of detecting the intersection of two or more objects. While the topic is most often associated with its use in video games and other physical simulations, it also has applications in robotics. In addition to determining whether two objects have collided, collision detection systems may also calculate time of impact (TOI), and report a contact manifold (the set of intersecting points).
Constraint	In mathematics, a constraint is a condition that a solution to an optimization problem must satisfy. There are two types of constraints: equality constraints and inequality constraints. The set of solutions that satisfy all constraints is called the feasible set.
Sorting algorithm	In computer science and mathematics, a sorting algorithm is an algorithm that puts elements of a list in a certain order. The most-used orders are numerical order and lexicographical order. Efficient sorting is important for optimizing the use of other algorithms (such as search and merge algorithms) that require sorted lists to work correctly; it is also often useful for canonicalizing data and for producing human-readable output.

Function object	A function object, functional, or functionoid, is a computer programming construct allowing an object to be invoked or called as though it were an ordinary function, usually with the same syntax.
	Description
	A typical use of a function object is in writing callback functions. A callback in procedural languages, such as C, may be performed by using function pointers.
Optimization	In mathematics, computer science and economics, optimization, refers to choosing the best element from some set of available alternatives.
	In the simplest case, this means solving problems in which one seeks to minimize or maximize a real function by systematically choosing the values of real or integer variables from within an allowed set. This formulation, using a scalar, real-valued objective function, is probably the simplest example; the generalization of optimization theory and techniques to other formulations comprises a large area of applied mathematics.

Chapter 5. NETWORKING

Peer-to-peer	Peer-to-peer computing or networking is a distributed application architecture that partitions tasks or work loads between peers. Peers are equally privileged, equipotent participants in the application. They are said to form a peer-to-peer network of nodes.
Berkeley sockets	The Berkeley sockets application programming interface (API) comprises a library for developing applications in the C programming language that perform inter-process communication, most commonly for communications across a computer network.
	Berkeley sockets originated with the 4.2BSD Unix operating system (released in 1983) as an API. Only in 1989, however, could UC Berkeley release versions of its operating system and networking library free from the licensing constraints of AT'T's copyright-protected Unix.
	The Berkeley socket API forms the de facto standard abstraction for network sockets.
Protocol	In object-oriented programming, a protocol is what or how unrelated objects use to communicate with each other. These are definitions of methods and values which the objects agree upon in order to cooperate.
	For example, in Java (where protocols are termed interfaces), the `Comparable` interface specifies a method `compareTo` which implementing classes should implement.
Shell	A shell is a piece of software that provides an interface for users of an operating system which provides access to the services of a kernel. However, the term is also applied very loosely to applications and may include any software that is 'built around' a particular component, such as web browsers and email clients that are 'shells' for HTML rendering engines. The name shell originates from shells being an outer layer of interface between the user and the internals of the operating system (the kernel).
Engine	An engine is a continuation-based construct that provides timed preemption. Engines which can contain other engines are sometimes called nesters and engines which don't have this ability are then called flat engines. To implement timed preemption there needs to be a clock.

Chapter 5. NETWORKING

Interface	In the field of computer science, an interface refers to a point of interaction between components, and is applicable at the level of both hardware and software. This allows a component, whether a piece of hardware such as a graphics card or a piece of software such as an internet browser, to function independently while using interfaces to communicate with other components via an input/output system and an associated protocol. In addition to hardware and software interfaces, a computing interface may refer to the means of communication between the computer and the user by means of peripheral devices such a monitor or a keyboard, an interface with the internet via Internet Protocol, and any other point of communication involving a computer.
Mersenne twister	The Mersenne twister is a pseudorandom number generator developed in 1997 by Makoto Matsumoto (?? ?$^?$) and Takuji Nishimura (?? ??$^?$) that is based on a matrix linear recurrence over a finite binary field F_2. It provides for fast generation of very high-quality pseudorandom numbers, having been designed specifically to rectify many of the flaws found in older algorithms. There are at least two common variants of the algorithm, differing only in the size of the Mersenne primes used.
Node	A node is an abstract basic unit used to build linked data structures such as trees, linked lists, and computer-based representations of graphs. Each node contains some data and possibly links to other nodes. Links between nodes are often implemented by pointers or references.
File Transfer Protocol	File Transfer Protocol is a standard network protocol used to copy a file from one host to another over a TCP/IP-based network, such as the Internet. File Transfer Protocol is built on a client-server architecture and utilizes separate control and data connections between the client and server applications, which solves the problem of different end host configurations (i.e., Operating System, file names). File Transfer Protocol is used with user-based password authentication or with anonymous user access.

Object model	In computing, object model has two related but distinct meanings:
	1. The properties of objects in general, in a specific computer programming language, technology, notation or methodology that uses them. For example, the Java object model, the COM object model, or the object model of OMT. Such object models are usually defined using concepts such as class, message, inheritance, polymorphism, and encapsulation. There is an extensive literature on formalized object models as a subset of the formal semantics of programming languages.
	2. A collection of objects or classes through which a program can examine and manipulate some specific parts of its world.
Taylor series	In mathematics, a Taylor series is a representation of a function as an infinite sum of terms that are calculated from the values of the function's derivatives at a single point.
	The concept of a Taylor series was formally introduced by the English mathematician Brook Taylor in 1715. he Scottish mathematician Colin Maclaurin, who made extensive use of this special case of Taylor series in the 18th century.
Optimization	In mathematics, computer science and economics, optimization, refers to choosing the best element from some set of available alternatives.
	In the simplest case, this means solving problems in which one seeks to minimize or maximize a real function by systematically choosing the values of real or integer variables from within an allowed set. This formulation, using a scalar, real-valued objective function, is probably the simplest example; the generalization of optimization theory and techniques to other formulations comprises a large area of applied mathematics.
Class	In object-oriented programming, a class is a construct that is used as a blueprint (or template) to create objects of that class. This blueprint describes the state and behavior that the objects of the class all share. An object of a given class is called an instance of the class.

Chapter 5. NETWORKING

Gateway

A gateway is a link between two computer programs or systems such as Internet Forums. A gateway acts as a portal between two programs allowing them to share information by communicating between protocols on a computer or between dissimilar computers.

Some examples of common gateways:

- E-mail <-> News server
- News server <-> Internet forum
- RSS aggregators <-> News server
- XMPP <-> ICQ

.

Index

In computer science, an index can be:

1. an integer which identifies an array element
2. a data structure that enables sublinear-time lookup

Array element identifier

When data objects are stored in an array, individual objects are selected by an index which is usually a non-negative scalar integer. Indices are also called subscripts.

There are three ways in which the elements of an array can be indexed:

0 (zero-based indexing)
    The first element of the array is indexed by subscript of 0.
1 (one-based indexing)
    The first element of the array is indexed by subscript of 1.
n (n-based indexing)
    The base index of an array can be freely chosen.

Chapter 5. NETWORKING

Navigation	Navigation is the process of monitoring and controlling the movement of a craft or vehicle from one place to another. It is also the term of art used for the specialized knowledge used by navigators to perform navigation tasks. All navigational techniques involve locating the navigator's position compared to known locations or patterns.
Age of Empires	Age of Empires is a series of computer games developed by Ensemble Studios and published by Microsoft Game Studios. The first title of the series was Age of Empires, released in 1997. Since then, seven titles and three spin-offs have been released. The titles are historical real-time strategy games, and their gameplay revolves around two main game modes: random map and campaign.
Synchronization	Synchronization is timekeeping which requires the coordination of events to operate a system in unison. The familiar conductor of an orchestra serves to keep the orchestra in time. Systems operating with all their parts in synchrony are said to be synchronous or in sync.
Clock synchronization	Clock synchronization is a problem from computer science and engineering which deals with the idea that internal clocks of several computers may differ. Even when initially set accurately, real clocks will differ after some amount of time due to clock drift, caused by clocks counting time at slightly different rates. There are several problems that occur as a repercussion of rate differences and several solutions, some being more appropriate than others in certain contexts.
Quicksort	Quicksort is a sorting algorithm developed by C. A. R. Hoare that, on average, makes $O(n\log n)$ (big O notation) comparisons to sort n items. In the worst case, it makes $O(n^2)$ comparisons, though if implemented correctly this behavior is rare. Typically, quicksort is significantly faster in practice than other $O(n\log n)$ algorithms, because its inner loop can be efficiently implemented on most architectures, and in most real-world data it is possible to make design choices that minimize the probability of requiring quadratic time.
Server	In computing, the term server is used to refer to one of the following: • a computer program running to serve the needs or requests of other programs (referred to in this context as 'clients') which may or may not be running on the same computer. • a physical computer dedicated to running one or more such services, to serve the needs of programs running on other computers on the same network. • a software/hardware system (i.e. a software service running on a dedicated computer) such as a database server, file server, mail server, or print server.

In computer networking, a server is a program that operates as a socket listener. The term server is also often generalized to describe a host that is deployed to execute one or more such programs.

A server computer is a computer, or series of computers, that link other computers or electronic devices together.

Numbers

Numbers is a spreadsheet application developed by Apple Inc. as part of the iWork productivity suite alongside Keynote and Pages. Numbers 1.0 was announced on August 7, 2007 and thus it is the newest application in the iWork Suite.

Compiler

A compiler is a computer program (or set of programs) that transforms source code written in a programming language (the source language) into another computer language (the target language, often having a binary form known as object code). The most common reason for wanting to transform source code is to create an executable program.

The name 'compiler' is primarily used for programs that translate source code from a high-level programming language to a lower level language (e.g., assembly language or machine code).

Inline function

In various versions of the C and C++ programming languages, an inline function is a function that the compiler has been requested to perform inline expansion upon. In other words, the programmer has requested that the compiler insert the complete body of the function in every place that the function is called, rather than generating code to call the function in the one place it is defined. (However, compilers are not obligated to respect this request).

Debugging

Debugging is a methodical process of finding and reducing the number of bugs, or defects, in a computer program or a piece of electronic hardware, thus making it behave as expected. Debugging tends to be harder when various subsystems are tightly coupled, as changes in one may cause bugs to emerge in another.

Origin

There is some controversy over the origin of the term 'debugging.'

The terms 'bug' and 'debugging' are both popularly attributed to Admiral Grace Hopper in the 1940s.

| Event | An event in the Unified Modeling Language (UML) is a notable occurrence at a particular point in time. |

Events can, but do not necessarily, cause state transitions from one state to another in state machines represented by state machine diagrams.

A transition between states occurs only when any guard condition for that transition are satisfied.

OpenMP

OpenMP is an application programming interface (API) that supports multi-platform shared memory multiprocessing programming in C, C++, and Fortran on many architectures, including Unix and Microsoft Windows platforms. It consists of a set of compiler directives, library routines, and environment variables that influence run-time behavior.

Jointly defined by a group of major computer hardware and software vendors, OpenMP is a portable, scalable model that gives programmers a simple and flexible interface for developing parallel applications for platforms ranging from the desktop to the supercomputer.

Algorithm

In mathematics, computer science, and other areas, an algorithm is an effective method for solving a problem expressed as a finite sequence of steps. Algorithms are used for calculation, data processing, and many other fields. .

Chapter 5. NETWORKING

Encryption	In cryptography, encryption is the process of transforming information (referred to as plaintext) using an algorithm (called cipher) to make it unreadable to anyone except those possessing special knowledge, usually referred to as a key. The result of the process is encrypted information (in cryptography, referred to as ciphertext). In many contexts, the word encryption also implicitly refers to the reverse process, decryption (e.g. 'software f' can typically also perform decryption), to make the encrypted information readable again (i.e. to make it unencrypted).
Initialization	In computer programming, initialization is the assignment of an initial value for a data object. The way how initialization is performed depends on programming language, as well as type, storage class, etc., of an object to be initialized. Programming constructs which perform initialization are typically called initializers and initializer lists.
Parameter	In computer programming, a parameter is a special kind of variable, used in a subroutine to refer to one of the pieces of data provided as input to the subroutine.. These pieces of data are called arguments. An ordered list of parameters is usually included in the definition of a subroutine, so that, each time the subroutine is called, its arguments for that call can be assigned to the corresponding parameters.
HMAC	In cryptography, HMAC is a specific construction for calculating a message authentication code (MAC) involving a cryptographic hash function in combination with a secret key. As with any MAC, it may be used to simultaneously verify both the data integrity and the authenticity of a message. Any cryptographic hash function, such as MD5 or SHA-1, may be used in the calculation of an HMAC; the resulting MAC algorithm is termed HMAC-MD5 or HMAC-SHA1 accordingly.
Processing	Processing is an open source programming language and integrated development environment (IDE) built for the electronic arts and visual design communities with the purpose of teaching the basics of computer programming in a visual context, and to serve as the foundation for electronic sketchbooks. The project was initiated in 2001 by Casey Reas and Ben Fry, both formerly of the Aesthetics and Computation Group at the MIT Media Lab. One of the stated aims of Processing is to act as a tool to get non-programmers started with programming, through the instant gratification of visual feedback.

Integer	In computer science, the term integer is used to refer to a data type which represents some finite subset of the mathematical integers. These are also known as integral data types. Value and representation The value of a datum with an integral type is the mathematical integer that it corresponds to.
Codec	A codec is a device or computer program capable of encoding and/or decoding a digital data stream or signal. The word codec is a portmanteau of 'compressor-decompressor' or, more commonly, 'coder-decoder'. A codec should not be confused with a coding or compression format or standard - a format is a document (the standard), a way of storing data, while a codec is a program (an implementation) which can read or write such files.
Collision	In computer science, a collision is a situation that occurs when two distinct pieces of data have the same hash value, checksum, fingerprint, or cryptographic digest. Collisions are unavoidable whenever members of a very large set (such as all possible person names, or all possible computer files) are mapped to a relatively short bit string. This is merely an instance of the pigeonhole principle.
Collision detection	Collision detection typically refers to the computational problem of detecting the intersection of two or more objects. While the topic is most often associated with its use in video games and other physical simulations, it also has applications in robotics. In addition to determining whether two objects have collided, collision detection systems may also calculate time of impact (TOI), and report a contact manifold (the set of intersecting points).

Index	In computer science, an index can be:
	1. an integer which identifies an array element
	2. a data structure that enables sublinear-time lookup
	Array element identifier
	When data objects are stored in an array, individual objects are selected by an index which is usually a non-negative scalar integer. Indices are also called subscripts.
	There are three ways in which the elements of an array can be indexed:
	0 (zero-based indexing)
	The first element of the array is indexed by subscript of 0.
	1 (one-based indexing)
	The first element of the array is indexed by subscript of 1.
	n (n-based indexing)
	The base index of an array can be freely chosen.
Class	In object-oriented programming, a class is a construct that is used as a blueprint (or template) to create objects of that class. This blueprint describes the state and behavior that the objects of the class all share. An object of a given class is called an instance of the class.
Optimization	In mathematics, computer science and economics, optimization, refers to choosing the best element from some set of available alternatives.
	In the simplest case, this means solving problems in which one seeks to minimize or maximize a real function by systematically choosing the values of real or integer variables from within an allowed set. This formulation, using a scalar, real-valued objective function, is probably the simplest example; the generalization of optimization theory and techniques to other formulations comprises a large area of applied mathematics.

Protocol	In object-oriented programming, a protocol is what or how unrelated objects use to communicate with each other. These are definitions of methods and values which the objects agree upon in order to cooperate.
	For example, in Java (where protocols are termed interfaces), the `Comparable` interface specifies a method `compareTo` which implementing classes should implement.
Block	In computer programming, a block is a section of code which is grouped together. Blocks consist of one or more declarations and statements. A programming language that permits the creation of blocks, including blocks nested within other blocks, is called a block structured programming language.
Event	An event in the Unified Modeling Language (UML) is a notable occurrence at a particular point in time.
	Events can, but do not necessarily, cause state transitions from one state to another in state machines represented by state machine diagrams.
	A transition between states occurs only when any guard condition for that transition are satisfied.
Channel	Channels are a tool used for interprocess communication. An object may be sent over a channel, and a process is able to receive any objects sent over a channel it has a reference to. They are similar to pipelines, but may contain arbitrary unserialised objects instead of lines of text, and are used within a single program for coordination, rather than across several programs.
Engine	An engine is a continuation-based construct that provides timed preemption. Engines which can contain other engines are sometimes called nesters and engines which don't have this ability are then called flat engines. To implement timed preemption there needs to be a clock.

Chapter 6. AUDIO

Speech recognition	Speech recognition converts spoken words to text. The term 'voice recognition' is sometimes used to refer to recognition systems that must be trained to a particular speaker--as is the case for most desktop recognition software. Recognizing the speaker can simplify the task of translating speech.
Mersenne twister	The Mersenne twister is a pseudorandom number generator developed in 1997 by Makoto Matsumoto (?? ?$^?$) and Takuji Nishimura (?? ??$^?$) that is based on a matrix linear recurrence over a finite binary field F_2. It provides for fast generation of very high-quality pseudorandom numbers, having been designed specifically to rectify many of the flaws found in older algorithms. There are at least two common variants of the algorithm, differing only in the size of the Mersenne primes used.
Implementation	Implementation is the realization of an application, idea, model, design, specification, standard, algorithm, or policy. In computer science, an implementation(computer science) · Programming language implementation · Algorithm · Application software · Code · Computation · Function · Method · Process · Proceeding · Procedure · Scheme

· Solution

· System

· Technique

'.

Arithmetic

arithmetic s is the oldest and most elementary branch of mathematics, used by almost everyone, for tasks ranging from simple day-to-day counting to advanced science and business calculations. It involves the study of quantity, especially as the result of combining numbers. In common usage, it refers to the simpler properties when using the traditional operations of addition, subtraction, multiplication and division with smaller values of numbers.

Data structure

In computer science, a data structure is a particular way of storing and organizing data in a computer so that it can be used efficiently.

Different kinds of data structures are suited to different kinds of applications, and some are highly specialized to specific tasks. For example, B-trees are particularly well-suited for implementation of databases, while compiler implementations usually use hash tables to look up identifiers.

Callback

In computer programming, a callback is a reference to executable code, or a piece of executable code, that is passed as an argument to other code. This allows a lower-level software layer to call a subroutine (or function) defined in a higher-level layer.

Use

Callbacks have a wide variety of uses.

Chapter 6. AUDIO

Polynomial	In mathematics, a polynomial is an expression of finite length constructed from variables (also known as indeterminates) and constants, using only the operations of addition, subtraction, multiplication, and non-negative integer exponents. For example, $x^2 - 4x + 7$ is a polynomial, but $x^2 - 4/x + 7x^{3/2}$ is not, because its second term involves division by the variable x (4/x) and because its third term contains an exponent that is not a whole number (3/2). The term 'polynomial' indicates a simplified algebraic form such that all polynomials are similarly simple in complexity (cf.
Synth	Synth is a skinnable Java look and feel, which is configured with an XML property file. According to Sun, goals for synth were: · Enable to create custom look without writing any code. · Allow appearance to be configured from images.
Object model	In computing, object model has two related but distinct meanings: 1. The properties of objects in general, in a specific computer programming language, technology, notation or methodology that uses them. For example, the Java object model, the COM object model, or the object model of OMT. Such object models are usually defined using concepts such as class, message, inheritance, polymorphism, and encapsulation. There is an extensive literature on formalized object models as a subset of the formal semantics of programming languages. 2. A collection of objects or classes through which a program can examine and manipulate some specific parts of its world.
Psychoacoustics	Psychoacoustics is the scientific study of sound perception. More specifically, it is the branch of science studying the psychological and physiological responses associated with sound (including speech and music). It can be further categorized as a branch of Psychophysics.

Chapter 6. AUDIO

Quicksort	Quicksort is a sorting algorithm developed by C. A. R. Hoare that, on average, makes O(nlogn) (big O notation) comparisons to sort n items. In the worst case, it makes $O(n^2)$ comparisons, though if implemented correctly this behavior is rare. Typically, quicksort is significantly faster in practice than other O(nlogn) algorithms, because its inner loop can be efficiently implemented on most architectures, and in most real-world data it is possible to make design choices that minimize the probability of requiring quadratic time.
Resampling	Resampling may refer to: • Resampling several related audio processes • Resampling resampling methods in statistics • Resampling scaling of bitmap images • Sample rate conversion .
Cache	In computer engineering, a cache is a component that transparently stores data so that future requests for that data can be served faster. The data that is stored within a cache might be values that have been computed earlier or duplicates of original values that are stored elsewhere. If requested data is contained in the cache this request can be served by simply reading the cache, which is comparatively faster. Otherwise (cache miss), the data has to be recomputed or fetched from its original storage location, which is comparatively slower. Hence, the more requests can be served from the cache the faster the overall system performance is.
Operator	Programming languages generally support a set of operators that are similar to operations in mathematics. A language may contain a fixed number of built-in operators (e.g. + - * = in C and C++), or it may allow the creation of programmer-defined operators (e.g. Haskell). Some programming languages restrict operator symbols to special characters like + or := while others allow also names like `div` (e.g. Pascal).
Surface	In mathematics, specifically in topology, a surface is a two-dimensional topological manifold. The most familiar examples are those that arise as the boundaries of solid objects in ordinary three-dimensional Euclidean space R^3 -- for example, the surface of a ball. On the other hand, there are surfaces, such as the Klein bottle, that cannot be embedded in three-dimensional Euclidean space without introducing singularities or self-intersections.
Library	In computer science, a library is a collection of resources used to develop software. These may include subroutines, classes, values or type specifications.

Libraries contain code and data that provide services to independent programs.

Template

Technical overview

There are two kinds of templates: function templates and class templates.

Function templates

A function template behaves like a function except that the template can have arguments of many different types . In other words, a function template represents a family of functions.

Feature

In computer vision and image processing the concept of feature is used to denote a piece of information which is relevant for solving the computational task related to a certain application. More specifically, features can refer to

- the result of a general neighborhood operation (feature extractor or feature detector) applied to the image,
- specific structures in the image itself, ranging from simple structures such as points or edges to more complex structures such as objects.

Other examples of features are related to motion in image sequences, to shapes defined in terms of curves or boundaries between different image regions, or to properties of such a region.

The feature concept is very general and the choice of features in a particular computer vision system may be highly dependent on the specific problem at hand.

Feature extraction

In pattern recognition and in image processing, feature extraction is a special form of dimensionality reduction.

When the input data to an algorithm is too large to be processed and it is suspected to be notoriously redundant (much data, but not much information) then the input data will be transformed into a reduced representation set of features . Transforming the input data into the set of features is called feature extraction.

Signal

In the fields of communications, signal processing, and in electrical engineering more generally, a signal is any time-varying or spatial-varying quantity.

In the physical world, any quantity measurable through time or over space can be taken as a signal. Within a complex society, any set of human information or machine data can also be taken as a signal.

Dynamic time warping

Dynamic time warping is an algorithm for measuring similarity between two sequences which may vary in time or speed. For instance, similarities in walking patterns would be detected, even if in one video the person was walking slowly and if in another he or she were walking more quickly, or even if there were accelerations and decelerations during the course of one observation. Dynamic time warping has been applied to video, audio, and graphics -- indeed, any data which can be turned into a linear representation can be analyzed with Dynamic time warping. A well known application has been automatic speech recognition, to cope with different speaking speeds.

Compiler

A compiler is a computer program (or set of programs) that transforms source code written in a programming language (the source language) into another computer language (the target language, often having a binary form known as object code). The most common reason for wanting to transform source code is to create an executable program.

The name 'compiler' is primarily used for programs that translate source code from a high-level programming language to a lower level language (e.g., assembly language or machine code).

Clam101

Chapter 6. AUDIO

Instance	In object-oriented programming an instance is an occurrence or a copy of an object, whether currently executing or not. Instances of a class share the same set of attributes, yet will typically differ in what those attributes contain. For example, a class 'Employee' would describe the attributes common to all instances of the Employee class.
Matching	In the mathematical discipline of graph theory, a matching is a set of edges without common vertices. It may also be an entire graph consisting of edges without common vertices. Given a graph G = (V,E), a matching M in G is a set of pairwise non-adjacent edges; that is, no two edges share a common vertex.
OpenMP	OpenMP is an application programming interface (API) that supports multi-platform shared memory multiprocessing programming in C, C++, and Fortran on many architectures, including Unix and Microsoft Windows platforms. It consists of a set of compiler directives, library routines, and environment variables that influence run-time behavior. Jointly defined by a group of major computer hardware and software vendors, OpenMP is a portable, scalable model that gives programmers a simple and flexible interface for developing parallel applications for platforms ranging from the desktop to the supercomputer.
Algorithm	In mathematics, computer science, and other areas, an algorithm is an effective method for solving a problem expressed as a finite sequence of steps. Algorithms are used for calculation, data processing, and many other fields. .
Constraint	In mathematics, a constraint is a condition that a solution to an optimization problem must satisfy. There are two types of constraints: equality constraints and inequality constraints. The set of solutions that satisfy all constraints is called the feasible set.
Macro	A macro in computer science is a rule or pattern that specifies how a certain input sequence (often a sequence of characters) should be mapped to an output sequence (also often a sequence of characters) according to a defined procedure. The mapping process that instantiates (transforms) a macro into a specific output sequence is known as macro expansion.

The term originated with macro-assemblers, where the idea is to make available to the programmer a sequence of computing instructions as a single program statement, making the programming task less tedious and less error-prone.

Method

In object-oriented programming, a method is a subroutine that is exclusively associated either with a class (in which case it is called a class method is an instance method). Like a subroutine in procedural programming languages, a method usually consists of a sequence of programming statements to perform an action, a set of input parameters to customize those actions, and possibly an output value (called the return value) of some kind. Methods provide a mechanism for accessing and manipulating the encapsulated data stored in an object.

Vorbis

Vorbis is a free software / open source project headed by the Xiph.Org Foundation (formerly Xiphophorus company). The project produces an audio format specification and software implementation (codec) for lossy audio compression. Vorbis is most commonly used in conjunction with the Ogg container format and it is therefore often referred to as Ogg Vorbis.

Inline function

In various versions of the C and C++ programming languages, an inline function is a function that the compiler has been requested to perform inline expansion upon. In other words, the programmer has requested that the compiler insert the complete body of the function in every place that the function is called, rather than generating code to call the function in the one place it is defined. (However, compilers are not obligated to respect this request).

9 781619 059887